Praise for

CAMERADO, I GIVE YOU MY HAND

"As you will learn in the pages of *Camerado, I Give You My Hand,* David T. Link is a remarkable man who has led an extraordinary life. There is much that we can learn from his wit, his wisdom, and his compassion for others." —**Sister Helen Prejean, author of** *Dead Man Walking* **and** *The Death of Innocents*

"Lawyer, dean of the Notre Dame Law School, husband, father, grandfather, widower, and now, Catholic priest. Father Dave Link's story is an inspiration and a challenge to us all. In his priesthood, Father Dave does more than just visit the incarcerated men he serves; he helps to truly transform their lives. *Camerado, I Give You My Hand* brings the story of this remarkable man and dedicated priest to life." —**Cardinal Timothy M. Dolan, Archbishop of New York and author of** *True Freedom*

"Who are the 'least' of our brothers and sisters, to use Jesus's own words? Surely among the most forgotten and least cared for are men and women behind bars, whose ranks grow every year. Often seen by many as undeserving of any sort of human care, indeed of any kind of attention, prison inmates are, in the Christian worldview, among the most deserving of pastoral care. The deeply moving story of Dr. David T. Link reminds us how God can be found anywhere, how Jesus makes himself known in surprising ways among the poor and marginalized, and why 'visiting the imprisoned' is one of the greatest of all works of mercy." —**James Martin, SJ, author of** *The Jesuit Guide to (Almost) Everything*

Camerado,

I Give You My Hand

WITH

A CRIME PEACE PLAN

BY

David T. Link

CAMERADO,
I GIVE YOU MY HAND

How a Powerful Lawyer-Turned-Priest Is

Changing the Lives of Men Behind Bars

MAURA POSTON ZAGRANS

IMAGE

New York

Copyright © 2013 by Maura Poston Zagrans

Published in the United States by Image,
an imprint of the Crown Publishing Group,
a division of Random House, Inc., New York.
www.crownpublishing.com

IMAGE is a registered trademark, and the "I" colophon
is a trademark of Random House, Inc.

Library of Congress Cataloging-in-Publication Data
Zagrans, Maura Poston.
    Camerado, I give you my hand : how a powerful lawyer-
turned-priest is changing the lives of men behind bars : with a
crime peace plan by Reverend David T. Link / Maura Poston
Zagrans.—First Edition.
        pages cm
    1. Church work with prisoners—Indiana. 2. Indiana State
Prison. I. Title.
    BV4340.Z34   2013
    282.092 B   2013000619

ISBN 978-0-385-34800-3
eISBN 978-0-385-34801-0

Printed in the United States of America

Cover design by Jessie Sayward Bright
Cover photography by Maura Poston Zagrans

10 9 8 7 6 5 4 3 2 1

First Edition

This book is dedicated with love and gratitude to

BARB and DAVE LINK,

who show us that happiness is ours when we join hands

with the least, the last, the lost, and the lonely

and make of them our camerados.

Contents

PART FOUR: CLARITY

Prison as Clarifier / 177

Coda / 221

Author's Note

I'll never forget the moment I first heard about David T. Link.

I was at the University of Notre Dame for a business meeting. I was introduced to Mary Nucciarone, whose longtime career as a financial aid official has given her a panoramic view of Notre Dame's leadership. Mary mentioned that Dave, who is the founding president of Notre Dame, Australia, as well as dean emeritus of the Notre Dame Law School, had recently become a priest. Known for his ardent championing of civil rights and for cofounding the Center for the Homeless in South Bend, Dave is also a dad and grandfather. Both he and his wife of forty-five years are beloved—and here, Mary became emphatic—by everyone. In 2003, just when Dave was all set to enjoy retirement, Barbara died of cancer. Five years later, Dave was ordained to the priesthood. Now in his seventies, he spends his days inside supermax-, maximum-, medium-, and minimum-security prisons, where he is changing lives.

I felt the zing of an arrow going straight into my author's heart.

"THAT'S A BOOK," I shouted.

I asked whether anyone had written a book about this man.

Mary tilted her head and considered my question. Awaiting her answer, I felt a wildness that bordered on panic. Finally, she gave the answer I was hoping to hear.

"I don't think so."

I knew in that moment that the telling of this story was my destiny.

It did not take long to arrange a first meeting. Father Dave and I talked, laughed, even shed a few tears over a breakfast that lasted three hours. There is a luminous quality about him, and I found it very distracting. This first impression has never been dispelled. I came to understand that the source of this incandescence is happiness.

In the beginning, one question drove my inquiry. I had to know:

Why, in the twilight years of a spectacularly successful life—precisely when he is able to dial it down from the frenetic pace he kept up for fifty years, when he finally has the time to relish his family, his friends, and his accomplishments—does a man put aside a life of ease to become a Catholic priest?

The answer to that question is both simple and complex. This book is that answer.

You are about to meet someone who has changed my life: Reverend David T. Link, whom I call Father Dave. Get ready. He just might change your life, too.

Father Dave upends what we think we know about mercy, compassion, justice, and service. He shows that even in the most fallow of fields the seeds of peace can be sown with the hand of friendship. He demonstrates how helping others can be the purpose of life as well as the joy in life. His faith is straightforward: love is a verb; everything else is just chatter.

Behind the razor wire, Father Dave seeks to connect with prisoners who have the potential to become camerados, people who are more than friends but less than dependents. Although he is happy to lend a hand, he refuses to engage in giving handouts. He will help people on their journey, but he will not make the journey for them; his expectation is that they desire and reach for the healing hand of love.

In ministering to men behind bars, Father Dave has chosen not to wait for these prodigal sons to have a change of heart, retrace their steps, and come find him. He has gone to where they are—to the steel-barred cells and guarded housing units where thousands upon thousands of human beings have been warehoused. Father Dave's immersion in the prison world has led him to understand that our criminal justice system is itself a kind of prodigal son, and he has written a comprehensive Crime Peace Plan that will save money, restore lives, and rescue the criminal justice system by returning it "home" to its original purpose, which is not to punish but rather to heal.

I have spent three years getting to know Father Dave and many of the people who have been touched by his life. In conducting research I was welcomed into some of the most privileged offices in the world of academe by men and women of letters. Father Dave's family, friends, faculty, and former students were gracious in entrusting me with their parts of his narrative. I also went behind The Wall to sit and talk with men who have been convicted of murder, assault and battery, armed robbery, various sex offenses, drug dealing, kidnapping, and more. All of us agree that Father Dave is extraordinary, and we see in his story an inspirational profile in courage that must be shared.

What began as a study of why one man would sacrifice the ease of his retirement years to improve the lives of people who are in dire straits underwent an evolution that, not surprisingly, mirrors a metamorphosis undergone by this attorney-at-law. "Along the way, things changed for me," admits Father Dave. "Before I got involved in prison ministry, I didn't think about or care what happened to people in prison. I guess I just assumed that they must be bad people or they wouldn't be in there. You know, 'You do the crime, you do the time.' And so it's a great surprise that God has chosen me for this career."

I was and am still mesmerized by someone whose happiness is so bottomless it seems to stand outside the normal parameters of time, place, and circumstance. And so this is neither a how-to nor a self-help book. Rather it is a story about one man's compassion that gives us a template for joy and fulfillment.

To know Father Dave is to be enriched in unexpected ways. One of the gifts he gave me was a keen appreciation for the unlimited potential in my life—indeed, in all of our lives. He validates the notion that there is no such thing as just one calling in life. Life is a series of callings.

What I hope to give you with my book is the potent insight and example Father Dave has provided for all of us: the great enemy of love is not hate, but indifference.

Preface

by

Sister Helen Prejean

Author of *Dead Man Walking* and *The Death of Innocents*

I first met the Reverend David T. Link in 2009. The two of us were being honored by the national chapter of Dismas House (dismas.org), an organization dedicated to facilitating successful reconnections between former prisoners and society. Dave graciously permitted me to deliver my (rather impassioned) acceptance remarks first. When I stepped from the dais, I noticed that there were tears in his eyes. At the conclusion of the formalities, Dave jokingly expressed some regret over his decision and gave me a compliment that I value to this day. He said that I was a tough act to follow and that he would never again give me first dibs on the microphone.

The truth is, Father Dave was being too modest. As you will learn in the pages of *Camerado, I Give You My Hand,* David T. Link is a remarkable man who has led an extraordinary life. There is much that we can learn from his wit, his wisdom, and his compassion for others.

In 2011, I was delighted to learn that Father Dave is not one to hold a grudge. Despite his (mock) grouchiness over my

Dismas House speech, there he was, seated in the second row of a packed auditorium at the University of Notre Dame where, under the sponsorship of the Center for Social Concerns, I spoke about justice as "just us." After the event, Father Dave and I were able to compare notes on the work that consumes our days.

I am heartened to have someone as accomplished, effective, and good-hearted as Father Dave as my colaborer in the vineyards of the criminal justice system. It is my hope that you will join us in our efforts to heal the broken systems in our society and tend to the people who are being crushed in their gears.

PART ONE

COURAGE

Camerado, I give you my hand!

I give you my love more precious than money,

I give you myself before preaching or law;

Will you give me yourself? will you come travel with me?

Shall we stick by each other as long as we live?

—WALT WHITMAN

"Song of the Open Road" from *Leaves of Grass*

Prison was not designed for who I am. It was designed for who I was.

—Jason Curry, prison resident, Indiana State Prison

One-Way Train Overture

An automated steel gate lurches, clumsy and clattering, like a massive antique elevator door, toward the wall. When the gate collides into the wall, the steel cell in which Reverend David T. Link is standing shudders. He hears the latching of the lock as the gate is secured, and then silence. He is momentarily caged while the steel grid in front of him is opened by corrections officers who work from a remote location. When he steps from the cage, Father Dave crosses over from "the outside" and into incarcerated territory behind The Wall at Indiana State Prison. It is a place in which not many people choose to be.

Indiana State Prison in Michigan City, Indiana, is a maximum-security facility that houses three categories of prisoners: violent offenders who have been convicted of crimes such as armed robbery, kidnapping, and serial killing; men who have been given long-term sentences for offenses that run the gamut from sex crimes to multiple driving offenses and trafficking in drugs; and people who have been condemned to death. More than 70 percent of Indiana State Prison's inmates are convicted murderers.

The facility is as old and unmovable as a mountain. In 1859

crowded conditions in Indiana's one and only prison prompted
the legislature to purchase one hundred acres of flat farmland in
the northern quadrant of the state, just a couple of miles from
Lake Michigan. A new prison was to be constructed on the site
to handle the overflow in the prison population. The first structure of what would become Indiana State Prison was built in
1860, President Abraham Lincoln's first inaugural year. It was
only two hundred feet long. Two years later it proved useful as
a prisoner-of-war facility for the rebel soldiers who were captured by the Yankees in the Civil War. From that single red brick
building the prison facility spread across the acreage, growing
over time into an imposing fortress of stark austerity.

Today Indiana State Prison dominates the landscape of a
community that seems to have surrendered. Neglected homes
and hollowed-out shells that once were stores and businesses sur-
round the prison like architectural carnage. The sheer enormity
of the complex is intimidating. A thirty-foot-high cement wall
prevents anyone from seeing into or out of the prison. This wall,
topped by ten-foot-high coils of razor wire, forms a perimeter
around a twenty-four-acre compound.

Inside the compound as many as twenty-four hundred men
live in four cell houses, two dormitories, and X Row, which is
the politically correct euphemism for what used to be called
death row. Fifty-some buildings, including a chapel and a firehouse, crowd the compound. A blacktop, two-direction driveway known as Main Street bisects the prison complex. Identical
white headstones stretch like dotted lines on a highway across a
cemetery in which hundreds of incarcerated men have been buried. Every sight line is punctuated by unnerving tangles of coiled

razor wire or by taut cables of barbed wire. Ten watchtowers loom over this fiercely guarded ghetto.

This is the place in which attorney-at-law, retired academic, and late-career priest Dave Link has chosen to spend his twilight years.

On this particular sultry mid-August Sunday morning, Father Dave has come to Indiana State Prison to celebrate Mass for Catholic prisoners. One last checkpoint, a narrow wooden guardhouse that resembles an old-fashioned covered footbridge, stands between the seventy-three-year-old priest and the chapel toward which he is heading. Stepping inside, he grins. "I haven't seen *you* in a while," he says to the corrections officer who is presiding at her post from behind a tall countertop. The woman's face lights up. She tells him what has been going on in her life while he presents for her inspection the liturgical robes and books he is carrying. She looks them over and waves him through.

With each brisk stride down the cement sidewalk leading to the chapel, the Indiana Department of Corrections identification tag swings like a pendulum from a blue lanyard Father Dave wears around his neck. Gold letters woven into the lanyard spell NOTRE DAME ALUMNI ASSOCIATION, a clue to his identity on the outside. He climbs a few cement steps, pulls on the handle of a wooden door, steps inside the chapel, and is slapped in the face by a bullying wall of humidity.

The cavernous, 6,905-square-foot chapel was constructed more than a century ago, designed for use as both a place of worship and a theater. Today religious services as well as special events such as observances of national holidays and appearances by comedians and musicians are held in this unair-conditioned space. Three hundred and eighty-six wooden seats are bolted to a painted cement floor that slopes from the back of the room to the foot of a large stage. Tall stained-glass windows stretch along both sides of the room, but they are dull and uninspiring. Grime and a black iron grid prevent the refraction of the sun's rays, rendering the glass mute.

Father Dave looks over the room in search of a remedy for the oppressive heat. Spotting some steel-framed industrial pedestal fans, he makes a mental note to ask some of the guys to plug them in and get the air circulating.

He moves down the long center aisle to the front of the room, crosses over to the right, and tucks typewritten notes for his homily into a shelf beneath the lectern. He places his red leather-bound Sacramentary, the book of prayers he follows in celebrating Mass, on a chair. He lays his white linen alb and white chasuble across the chair back. As he dons the liturgical garments that are worn by Roman Catholic priests all over the world on this Sunday morning, he recites the vesting prayers silently.

Fully dressed to celebrate Mass, he takes up a post in front of the first row of seats. Standing with his palms pressed together, he rests his chin on his thumbs and his forefingers against his lips. He gazes toward the back of the room and becomes still as a statue. Any moment now, the prodigal sons he awaits will be coming through the door on which he is training his gaze.

The stillness is shattered as the door is flung wide. A very large man bursts through the doorway. Two steps inside, he slams on the brakes and scans the chapel. Fluorescent lights glinting off his spectacles create white rectangles where his eyes should be. Father Dave recognizes the burly figure in an instant. A smile lifts his face, and he calls out to the khaki-clad prisoner.

"Jeff!"

His booming baritone voice provides Jeffrey Krumm the focal point he is seeking, and Jeff charges down the middle aisle. At six feet five inches and weighing more than three hundred pounds, he moves with a lightness that belies his size. Jeff's boisterous handshake gives way to a bear hug.

"It's so good to see you, Doc."

"It's great to see you, brother."

Jeff unwraps his arms so he can stand back and get a good look at the man who changed his life.

People meeting Father Dave for the first time often have a strong impression that there is something about him that is familiar. He seems a hybrid of two well-known American figures, Emmy Award–winning late-night television talk show host Johnny Carson and "king of golf" Arnold Palmer. Like Carson, Father Dave is quick-witted, and his dimples and merry eyes punctuate a face that is always expressive, often comical. But Father Dave's broad forehead, wisps of hair that tend to wander from their assigned places, and guilelessness evoke the gentlemanly Palmer.

"Less than two weeks till the home opener, Doc. Purdue."

Jeff never fails to trade talk about his beloved Fighting Irish teams with Father Dave. Both men share a passion for all things Notre Dame. Before he was incarcerated, Jeff worked as a security guard in the student section of the Notre Dame Stadium. Father Dave is a double-Domer—both his undergraduate and law degrees were earned at Notre Dame. He was the founding president of the University of Notre Dame, Australia and served as dean of the University of Notre Dame Law School for twenty-four years.

"You'll be there, won't you?" Jeff attends the games vicariously through Father Dave, and the postgame biopsies they conduct are a high point of his week.

"You know I wouldn't miss it," Father Dave replies, and they jump right into an assessment of the starting lineup.

Soon staccato clangs coming in quick succession signal the arrival of several dozen more prisoners who have hurried to the chapel from their housing units. Some collect hymnals and missals and take a seat. Some talk with one another or with volunteers from local parishes who visit as part of a prison outreach ministry. Most, however, make a beeline for the priest with the mischievous grin.

Father Dave is a man of many monikers. Each is a tip-off for when a prisoner first met Father Dave as well as how close their relationship is. To most prison administrators and correctional officers, then, he is Chaplain Link. After some inmates learned that he has four doctoral degrees they dubbed him Doc. To "lifers" who attended the correctional education courses he taught in the early 1990s, when he still was dean of Notre Dame Law School, he is Dean Link. To recent converts and new arrivals, he is Father Link. To those who consider him a close friend, those who were accustomed to calling him Dave before he was ordained a priest in 2008, he is Father Dave. And to thousands of men who live in eight of the twenty adult prison facilities in the state of Indiana, he is Brother.

As the prisoners cluster around their priest, Father Dave looks into each man's eyes, greets him by name, asks how he is doing, and then listens for the answer.

As the hour nears eleven, two prisoners, David Parrish and William R. "Bill" Dixon, arrange pages on their music stands and take some practice runs through their chords on the electric guitars that Father Dave purchased and donated to the chapel. Thirty-nine-year-old David Parrish is attractive, but his features are veiled by sadness. A philosopher by nature, David is a shy observer. He peers out from behind a thick and wavy mane that spills forward over his brow. Bill Dixon, whose strong, square jaw and erect bearing project self-assurance and self-control, views the world with equanimity from behind clear green eyes. Lean and rugged, the forty-six-year-old looks like a displaced wrangler, as if he should be dressed in Levis and chaps and saddling his horse for a cattle roundup.

Bill takes his eyes off of his sheet music. He searches for Father Dave and finds him encircled like a quarterback in a huddle. A pensive expression washes over Bill's face.

The road to incarceration has been long and torturous for every person in this facility. Three out of four are serving time for a murder conviction. Bill's path to Indiana State Prison involved not murder but an anguished and protracted disintegration of self. He offers a thumbnail sketch of his life.

"I was the kind of kid who was Grampa's favorite. The kid who could do no wrong. I can't remember a time when I wasn't dreaming of being a musician, and then I got my first guitar and started playing at the age of—what, thirteen? Fourteen? Then I grew up, and I got married, and she was the most beautiful wife ever. And we had a son, and he was the most amazing little boy I'd ever imagined. I had it *all*. And I threw it all away. I started getting high. I got addicted to cocaine. I let cocaine take them away."

Drugs thrust Bill into a lifestyle that led to years of criminal activity. After his wife divorced him, Bill figured that he already had one foot over the edge so he might as well go all the way. He was destined for a crash landing.

One night Bill robbed a store for cash and fled to a contiguous county. Armed with a gun, he burst into a house. He ordered the woman inside to put him and her son inside the trunk of her car and then drive through the roadblocks that had been set up by law enforcement. After she had driven them beyond the barricades, she was to pull over to the side of the road and let Bill and the boy out of the trunk. Bill drove away in the vehicle, leaving the mother and son by the side of the road. Walking until they found help, the two survived the ordeal physically unharmed but psychologically traumatized. Bill was convicted of robbery, resisting law enforcement, and two counts of kidnapping. He was sentenced to two consecutive sentences for a total of seventy-six and a half years.

It took coming to Indiana State Prison to shock Bill into sobriety. As soon as he arrived, he says, that was it for him.

Bill was a resident at Indiana State Prison in the early 1990s when Dean Link first started coming to the prison as a guest lecturer. Bill credits Father Dave with helping him grow up, be a man, and put his life into perspective. Does he have regrets? Of course. Can he change the past? Of course not. But having a relationship with someone who models honesty and accountability showed Bill how to accept responsibility for what he had done wrong—and then move on. Father Dave introduced Bill to the concept that everyone, even a guy in prison, has a purpose in life. It was unfortunate that Bill had to come to prison to be exposed to concepts of personal destiny and personal worth, but Bill carries himself with dignity now that he understands that it is not too late to get it right. After all, as he has learned from Father Dave, nothing less than eternity is at stake.

Bill's father died when he was a child of nine, and he freely admits to wishing that he had been blessed with a father like Dave Link. He says, "I wouldn't be in this place if I had." Sitting beside his fellow musician with a guitar cradled on his lap, Bill looks across the room at Father Dave and says to nobody in particular, "Every time I see that man, it makes me want to be his son."

Bill's mood is lifted when Father Dave glances over and aims one of his upside-down smiles, the double-dimpled one where his mouth forms an inverted U, toward the musicians. Bill tilts his head toward David and says, "Who else smiles like that? Nobody but him."

At 11:00 A.M., the prisoners wrap up their conversations and scatter to their seats. Father Dave has moved to the back of the room. Deacon John Bacon, the prisoners who will serve as lectors, and the prisoners who are altar servers line up two abreast in front of the priest. Father Dave looks to the musicians, gives them a nod, and Bill and David begin strumming their guitars. Altar server Jason Garver grasps a brass pole on top of which is mounted a crucifix, steps forward, and the procession begins.

As he walks up the aisle, Father Dave looks from one side of the chapel to the other, establishing eye contact with some of the prisoners. Details of their personal narratives come to him in a rush. To the left is the guy who broke down when Father Dave, envelope in hand, paid a call to his prison cell to wish him a happy birthday. The man had wept because Father Dave's was the first birthday card he had ever received.

To the right is a man whom Father Dave had counseled through a devastating event. One of the duties of prison chaplains is to let the incarcerated know when someone in the family has died. Of the many death notifications that Father Dave has delivered, none was more difficult than telling this particular man that his mother had been murdered. The prisoner asked if he would be able to attend his mother's funeral, and it was tough telling him that this could not happen, not even if he were to wear shackles. Father Dave consoled him by promising that if the funeral could be taped they would watch the video together over in the chapel. But Father Dave dreaded what was next, for he had yet to convey the worst of the news. The suspect that the police had arrested was the prisoner's father. Father Dave sat there in the cell as a mother's son crumbled. When it was time for the priest to go, the prisoner asked for a favor. He asked for a hug. Seeing this prisoner now, Father Dave feels that embrace reverberating in his heart.

The procession reaches the space that would have been used as the orchestra pit in days long gone. Father Dave bows before the altar upon which, only minutes earlier, Jason arranged candles, linen cloths, a chalice, and the Sacramentary. Father Dave turns to the congregants of the St. Dismas Community, so named by the prisoners after the "good thief" who called out to Jesus from the cross upon which he himself was hanging, and throws his arms open wide in a formal greeting to begin the liturgy.

It is August 15, the Roman Catholic Feast of the Assumption of the Blessed Virgin, which marks the taking up of Mary's body into heaven at the end of her earthly life. Father Dave has crafted the homily around this event. One cardinal rule he observes in writing his homilies is that each takes no more than six minutes.

Jeff Krumm says that he anticipates Father Dave's homilies with as much eagerness as he looks forward to phone calls from home. "The first time I heard Doc give a homily, it seemed to me that I was the only guy in the room. Years later I still feel that way. And every time he gives a homily, he gives a slam dunk."

After the introductory rites and the readings, it is time for Father Dave to give his sermon. The chapel is steamy and the men are still. Father Dave walks to the lectern, gives his notes a quick review, looks out upon his congregation, and begins.

"We all have a human mother who gave us birth, of course. In some cases, there is another human mother who raised us."

Around the room, heads are nodding.

"But we also have a spiritual mother who watches over us every day, no matter where we are."

Long pause.

"Even *here*."

He sketches what little facts are known about the mother of Jesus. She was a young girl, he says, and she lived in a backwater village, a place of poverty and little education.

"In essence, our spiritual mother was a teenager from the ghetto. And she had a tough life."

He lists some of the hardships that Mary knew.

"Today we celebrate the solemnity of this woman being taken directly into heaven. And we wonder, Why? Why did God take Mary directly into heaven?

"Think about it. This was his mom. And He had the power, so, why not? Maybe He wanted to save Mary from the sorrow of death. That's probably part of it. It may have been to reward Mary for having endured great sorrow in her lifetime. That's probably also a part of it.

"But most likely God assumed Mary into heaven because He wants us to know *for sure* that our spiritual mother is in heaven, where she is caring for us. Be assured that *right now* Mary is looking down on this chapel with pride and love for all who have come to honor her son."

At this point his shoulders drop, he steps back, and his voice takes on a new tone.

"To me it is amazing how little of what Mary said has been captured in Scripture. Perhaps the most famous are the words she spoke at the wedding feast at Cana. She told the servants, 'Do whatever He tells you.'

"Her advice was meant not just for the servers at a wedding reception. Her advice applies to all of us who are the spiritual sons and daughters of Mary."

Father Dave scans the chapel. When he is satisfied that he has made eye contact with as many upturned faces as possible, he says, "Do whatever He tells you."

He tucks his notes back into the shelf, folds his hands, and returns to his chair, where he sits during a brief period of silent reflection.

Jeff glances at his watch and smiles. Just under six minutes.

Jeff says that Father Dave's homilies give him food for thought that lasts throughout the coming week. "I know there's a world of knowledge in that man's head, and so you better believe I'm paying attention to what he has to say."

Jeff blames no one but himself for the disgrace and disappointment he has caused his family. He credits Father Dave for the moral maturity and sense of accountability he has attained since he was imprisoned at Indiana State Prison. He says that Father Dave helped him to see that it was his own narcissism that had prevented him from being able to admit to and seek help for a personality disorder that would lead to his incarceration. Jeff says, "Not a week goes by that I don't request advice from Doc. I found in him a friend that I can trust. He is a confidant and he is a brother to me. He changed my life by bringing me around to the idea that my life is worthwhile, and it is not too late to amend my life."

Thirty-six-year-old Todd Anderson was also listening to Father Dave's homily with rapt attention. "I was adopted," says Todd. "Last year at around Christmastime my parents lifted me up after they made a statement that they were sorry they didn't give the love that they should have given to me and my sister.

"If you are in need or hurting, there should be someone you can go to. That's how I see Mary. Even though I never knew my real mom, and that kind of hurts, Mary has opened up my heart to my real mother and to praying for her. One day, if my mom is still alive, I would like for us to cross paths and sit down as mother and son and talk.

"But I know that Mary is looking down on us and that we are her own children."

As if the thought has just occurred to him, Todd adds, "You know, in the Bible Jesus never called her 'Mother.' That's because he wanted us to know that we're hers, too."

Todd says that Father Dave has changed his life in two ways. First, Father Dave brought an element of reality to his concept of love. "He is so caring. He has such a loving heart. I used to think it was just words, but now, through him, I really do feel God's love. And I feel more at peace."

Second, Father Dave helped Todd become a better member of his community. "I used to be a very violent person," Todd confesses. "I didn't care about anything. I wouldn't ever ask forgiveness of anyone. But now if I do have a little burst of anger I have the heart and the courage to go to that individual and ask forgiveness, and explain what happened, and apologize. And it all comes around to the inspiration that I get from Doc. I'm so touched by him. He's like a great-granddad—a high-priority person that I look up to. He is a true father to me."

Whatever their personal histories might be, by the way that he addresses them Father Dave sends a clear message that he is expecting the best they can offer. To Father Dave these men are not inmates or prisoners; they are residents. They are not felons; they are former felons. They are, he says, his brothers. It means the world to the prisoners, all of whom are reluctant to talk about their pasts and many of whom would rather be judged based on the people they have become, that Father Dave treats them with this kind of civility.

Anthony Wheeler, whose good looks and elocution call to mind the actor Sidney Poitier, explains, "Dr. Link thinks of us as people. He has an uncanny ability to sense what we need without being told. He has a genuine concern for me—for my emotional and my physical well-being. He introduces me to people as 'my brother, ex-felon Anthony Wheeler.' "

By design, prison life is lonely. Anthony has spent many hours of his incarceration writing poetry. In his poems Anthony examines motifs such as family, friendship, solitude, and love, and he has collected some of his work in an unpublished volume entitled "From the Inside Out Comes Poetry from Within." He says that Father Dave has helped him attain a state of mind in which he is better able to tolerate the unrelenting solitariness of long-term imprisonment.

"Dr. Link is a presence even when he is not here," he says. "I read a poem about how we are born alone and we die alone, and that everything in between is a gift from God. Father Link has no idea what impact he's had on my life. But his presence—the fact that he is here—takes away my feeling of being alone."

In the closing rites Father Dave announces that immediately following the conclusion of Mass, David Parrish and Bill Dixon will play a new song that David has written, and that everyone is welcome to stay and enjoy the performance. Father Dave blesses the people, venerates the altar, and falls into line behind the other ministers. After the last verse of the recessional hymn is sung, Father Dave hurries back to the front of the room. He looks over the chapel. Seeing that everyone is still seated, he smiles like a proud papa. Then he turns his full attention on the two musicians.

Bill, who also writes music and who sounds uncannily like Pearl Jam's Eddie Vedder, is usually the lead singer but today Bill will sing harmony on David's song, "Discovery Through the Ashes."

David is tenuous as he sings the opening lines.

> *The sun goes down a little early*
> *to chase away the afternoon*
> *I do my best not to worry*
> *about the hell that I've been through.*

He takes a peek at Father Dave before singing the refrain.

> *'Cause I'm leavin' on a one-way train*
> *picking up pieces that I've misplaced*
> *scattered through the ashes*
> *but in my hands, in my hands are the matches.*

Not one prisoner has moved from his seat as David plunges into the second verse.

> *I feel my heart beating faster*
> *drawing close to the end*
> *And my mind won't lay still*
> *from all the madness within.*

'Cause I'm leavin' on a one-way train
picking up pieces that I've misplaced
scattered through the ashes
but in my hands, in my hands are the matches.

The guitars hush during the bridge.

And what's left now when we're broken down
and there's nothing left to break?
But look at how, look at how we've changed!

The guitars fill the room in a mighty crescendo, yet it is David's lyrics that hold sway.

I find myself drawing closer
to the One who believes in me
And God I hope that there's forgiveness,
a place for me somewhere up there
And God I hope we have the courage
to be the one we know we should be.

'Cause we're leavin' on a one-way train
picking up pieces that we've misplaced
scattered through the ashes
but in our hands, in our hands are the matches.

The audience breaks out into applause so intense that David does not dare look up. Beside him Bill is nodding approvingly, and from across the room Father Dave is beaming. The prisoners are still clapping as, mindful of being in their cells for the mandatory 2:00 head count, they rise from their seats and disperse to their housing units.

The performance has left the chapel workers with less time than they normally have to disassemble the altar props, guitars, and sound equipment. At fifteen minutes to the hour, the prisoners are hurrying to get everything put away. At ten minutes to the hour, everyone has vanished, Brigadoon-like, and an eerie silence rings in Father Dave's ears.

He will be back tomorrow morning to visit with the men one-on-one in their housing units, but now it is time to go home. He checks to be sure that the storage closets in which the linens, candlesticks, candles, paten, and chalice have been put away are locked. Shadows descend as Father Dave flips switches on the light panel and the fluorescent bulbs are doused. Scooping up his Sacramentary, alb, and chasuble, he takes one last look around before he pushes the door open and steps outside. He finds the correct key on a jangly key ring and locks the door behind him. Then he turns and takes a moment to lift his face to the sun.

Setting off toward Main Street, he walks past a flagpole that boasts the black POW/MIA flag as well as the Stars and Stripes. Across the driveway, three-story-high cyclone fencing topped with coiled razor wire divides barren land into exercise squares. A few men are in the yards. Spotting Father Dave, they call to him and move toward the fence. Father Dave grins. He crosses over and greets each man by name. He stands there talking with

them for a while, his fingers resting on diamond-shaped alumi-
num fencing. From high above, inside guard towers that glower
darkly against a bleached denim sky, shadowy figures holding
weapons bend toward the scene.

After saying good-bye, Father Dave walks from Main Street
to the sidewalk that will lead him in reverse order through the
same security routine he cleared earlier that morning. Inside the
Administration Building, the captain comes out from behind
his desk to check Father Dave's belongings. Moving through a
catacomb-like passageway, Father Dave passes a security booth
that sits up on a pedestal like an old-fashioned movie theater box
office; it is there that staff, nothing but faint shadows behind
the darkened windows, hold the driver's licenses of volunteers
while they are inside the prison. The final barrier to the outside
is unlocked remotely. Emerging from the subdued lighting, Father Dave is assaulted by the fluorescent glare of the lobby. To
his right, corrections officers reporting for the second shift are
enduring pat-downs and full-body scans. Father Dave waves to
the busy security officers and heads for freedom. Pushing open a
heavy glass door, he steps outside, stands at the top of the stairs,
and takes a deep, cleansing breath.

When one of his former faculty members asked why he had
not retired from academe to relax, travel, and play golf, Father
Dave, who once carried an eleven handicap, answered, "I want to
go out swinging a different kind of club. For years I volunteered
wearing a shirt and tie. Now I do it wearing a clerical collar. To
the vast majority of these men, most of whom have never had a
male role model, I have become a spiritual father and a surrogate
father. And I feel like I'm at the top of my game."

Father Dave tells people on the outside that in ministering to prisoners, he meets individuals who are incarcerated "not because they fell into the cracks of society. These people were born in the cracks." If his statement is met with raised eyebrows, he explains, "Almost all of the men I counsel grew up in fatherless homes. Most of them have suffered physical, emotional, or sexual abuse. Almost all are victims of crushing poverty, and of the poor education that comes with that. Fully 60 to 75 percent of this nation's prisoners are illiterate. It makes sense: If you can't read, you fall behind in school. If you fall behind in school, you will probably drop out. In fact, there is a direct correlation between failure to graduate from high school and the likelihood of being incarcerated."

For a country that prides itself on being "the land of the free," it is ironic that America incarcerates more of her citizenry than does any other country. Her penal system is the largest in the world. More tax dollars are spent on corrections than on education. The majority of Father Dave's brothers are socially marginal minorities who entered the prison system already powerless, jobless, and unaware of their purpose in life. The two-thirds recidivism rate in the United States is the worst in the world. Some of the old-timers confided that they have noticed a new trend: people are coming into the system at increasingly younger ages. Father Dave overheard one of the lifers asking a fish, that is, someone new to the prison, "What are you doing in here? Shouldn't you be going to the prom?" Another lifer who has been at Indiana State Prison for twenty years vents, "Delinquents—all they want to do is lock them up. Everyone has told these guys to find a job, get an education, learn a trade. But they come *in* with no trade and they *leave* with no trade. It's no wonder they come right back. They say it's a Department of Corrections but it's really a Department of Punishment."

Father Dave's prison ministry takes him inside eight of the state's twenty adult facilities, and they run the gamut from the lowest level of prisoner confinement to the highest.

People ask, "Are you ever afraid?"

He answers, "No."

How can this be?

First of all, that the prisoners cherish him is obvious. A conversation between Father Dave and one of the prisoners is indicative. The prisoner asked if Father Dave was interested in knowing what the guys at Indiana State Prison thought of him.

Father Dave nodded.

"We would give up our lives for you."

After an emotional pause, Father Dave asked, "Well, do you guys feel the same way about the other chaplain?"

"Absolutely," deadpanned the prisoner. "We'd give up his life for you, too."

Though he is touched by the prisoners' love and protectiveness, Father Dave says that there is a different reason that he feels no fear.

"The truth is," he explains, "I never walk alone. When I go into the prisons, two go with me. The Holy Spirit. And Barbara."

Barbara.

For Father Dave, saying her name is like praying a one-word prayer.

In the early centuries, it was not uncommon for Roman Catholic priests to be married. The Second Lateran Council in 1139 marked the prohibition of the ordination of married men. Even so, since that time the Church has allowed exceptions to the rule. Hence, in the twenty-first century, of America's nearly forty thousand Roman Catholic priests, there are approximately eighty married clergymen, most of whom were leaders of Episcopal or Anglican congregations before they joined the Catholic Church. Many of these priests have families.

Father Dave was not married when he was ordained. But he is a member of another subset of Catholic clergy. Father Dave is a widower priest.

For forty-five years Barbara Ann Winterhalter Link was Dave's wife and camerado. Father Dave says that she knew him better than he knew himself, so he trusted her without qualification. That is why when she first suggested that he become a prison volunteer he could revise his initial reaction.

They were sitting at the dining room table in their house in South Bend, Indiana. Out of the blue, Barbara said, "Dave, I think you should start lecturing over at Indiana State Prison."

"*Barbara.* Why would I want to go and lecture at the prison? I've just devoted most of my career to training people in the defense and prosecution of the prisoners who are *in* there. Now you want me to go and give lectures to people who've been convicted? No way."

"Well, you're a good teacher," she said. "And I just think you'd like it, that's all."

To Dave, her suggestion made no sense. On the other hand, Barbara's advice had always been reliable.

Dave contacted Ed Buss, who was then the superintendent of Indiana State Prison, and volunteered his help as a visiting professor.

Dave gave a series of three lectures on law and ethics to the Lifer's Group. Each session was packed to capacity. No guards were present in the classroom while Dave led the prisoners in discussions about the concept and philosophy of justice.

After finishing the lecture series, Dave was a different man. The experience made him question some of his assumptions about the American legal system. He had believed that the legal system was working as it was supposed to work. But meeting so many men who had been sentenced to life in prison for such vastly different kinds of crimes prodded him out of his complacency. How could it be, for example, that three men, one a drug user, another a drug dealer, and the third a murderer, had *all* received life sentences?

Dave was impressed at how hungry the prisoners were for knowledge that was not practical; they did not focus on information that would help them maneuver the legal system. Instead their questions were philosophical. They wanted to know not the *what* but the *why*. He had gone to Indiana State Prison believing that he would prove Barbara wrong, but after the conclusion of the lecture series, Dave felt as if he had been called to the prison to be a missionary of hope.

Eric Stahl, a member of the General Christian Assembly who would later join the Catholic community, was one of the first prisoners whose life was changed when Dean Link came on the scene. For twenty years Eric's job in the chapel had put him in a position to watch many chaplains come and go. He says that Dave's evolution from layperson to volunteer to chaplain has been uniquely inspirational.

"I was really tickled when Dave went through the seminary," recalls Eric. "Through the years he has become my personal friend. Now he is my pastor, my boss, my friend, my brother. We have great talks with each other. He'll tell you, 'You're wrong,' and I like that.

"This is not a pretty place. We're at the bottom of the barrel. Society looks at us as the stuff you scrape off your feet. But Doc chose to see what God sees in us.

"It's his heart. It's who he is—his character and his honesty.

"I witnessed many incidents that showed me what kind of person Doc is. One of them happened when he was in training, not yet a priest. One of the other chaplains ordered Doc to go get him some lunch. In the first place, it was ninety-five degrees outside. And here was this other, younger man being disrespectful to *Doc*. I was mad, but Doc showed no emotion. He showed humility. He humbled himself and served the other man.

"But *look out* if he sees someone *else* being abused.

"I saw someone being very unkind to a woman who worked as a secretary. She was elderly—she might have been in her early eighties but I'm not sure. Anyway, I saw Doc motion to this person who had been rude—abusive, really—and the two of them went into the Peace Room. The door was closed. Things felt a little different when they came out. I know this: I never saw that sweet old lady being treated like that again.

"The thing is, we know that Doc is here because he wants to be. This is not a job. It's a calling. He really cares about us.

One time I told him, 'No one is ever going to hurt you in this place. This prison isn't big enough for any man to hide if he ever hurts you. In fact, the whole country isn't big enough for anyone to hide in because we have connections.' But the fact is, no one wants to hurt him.

"And he's leading men to God. It used to be eight or ten men coming to Mass, but now the place is filling up. The head of the Latin Kings or the head of the Mexican Mafia and the head of the Asatrus—they all show him respect. Whatever gang somebody may be affiliated with, they recognize Doc as the real thing."

Eric was attending a prison college graduation ceremony during which he was going to be awarded a bachelor's degree when he learned of Dean Link's professional identity on the outside.

"Until that day I had no idea who Dave was," Eric recalls. "I would never have dreamt that he was dean of Notre Dame Law School."

Eric says that he will be forever grateful to Barbara for her role in bringing Dave into his life.

"Barbara. She sent him to us. I would have loved to have met her. I would have loved to have thanked her."

With a merciless sun blazing high overhead, gravel crunches beneath black Bostonian loafers as Father Dave walks through the parking lot to his car. He is thinking about his brothers. He feels unsettled, as if something is calling for his attention. Was there to be something more to this late-in-life career as a widower priest than just this prison ministry?

He pushes the remote unlock, pulls open the right rear

passenger door, and places his vestments and Sacramentary on the backseat. He swings the door closed. Head bowed and eyes cast to the ground, he crosses to the driver's side of the car, all the while trying to understand just what Barbara is asking of him now.

> *"First of all,"* he said, *"if you can learn a simple trick, Scout, you'll get along a lot better with all kinds of folks. You never really understand a person until you consider things from his point of view—"*
>
> *"Sir?"*
>
> *"—until you climb into his skin and walk around in it."*
>
> —Harper Lee, *To Kill a Mockingbird*

1. SETTING THE STAGE

Born in Sandusky, Ohio, on August 24, 1936, Dave was the youngest of Frank and Amelia Link's six children. When his parents brought Dave home from the hospital, there was plenty of built-in babysitting. Mary Jeanne was fifteen; Bud was fourteen; Dorothy, known to almost everyone as Dody, was eleven; Larry was eight; and little Frank was six years old. For Dave, who was raised in a Cleaver-esque family in small-town America, not even a bout with polio could dispel his perception of having had an idyllic childhood.

At the age of four, Dave was diagnosed as having rheumatic fever, but subsequently it was discovered that he had nonparalytic poliomyelitis. Dave's legs were so weakened by the polio that he changed from a robust, active little boy to an invalid. Dave recalls hearing the pediatrician telling his parents that their son would be lucky to be able to walk. Certainly, the doctor added, their child would never be able to run.

For one year, Frank came home from work several times

throughout the day so that he could carry Dave from one room into another. Dave spent his time playing with small toy cars and his baseball card collection. Whether he was on the couch or in his bed, stacks of children's books were always scattered in a semicircle around him. Dody found her calling as a nurse taking care of the little brother she had adored since the day he was born. Whenever she was not in school, she could be found hovering nearby. Frank and Amelia exercised Dave's atrophied legs daily. A little more than a year after he was diagnosed with polio, Dave was once again able to stand on his legs and practice walking. What Dave gained from the experience is a tremendous awareness of having been treasured, cared for, and loved.

By the time Dave was a teenager, his siblings were well into their adult lives. For Frank and Amelia, having David in the house when they otherwise would have had an empty nest was a blessing.

A knee injury Dave suffered playing ninth-grade football resulted in the discovery of a hidden talent. Running was prescribed as part of the program to rehabilitate his knee. The assistant football coach, who was trying to put together a track team, saw Dave running the hurdles inside the gym and asked Dave if he would go out to the track and pace the miler—that is, set a fast pace for the guy who would be their star runner. Although Dave thought he would not even be able to complete a mile, he complied. At each quarter mile Dave was surprised to discover not only that he could keep going but that the other boy was lagging farther and farther behind. That one trial convinced the coach that Dave Link should run the mile for the new St. Mary's

Catholic High School track team. Dave excelled in his new sport. All throughout high school and college he made good use of the legs that polio could have destroyed. He also continued to run in his adult years.

During his high school years, whenever practice for that season's sport (football, basketball, or track) was over, Dave would often walk from St. Mary's to his father's place of employment, Smith Motor Sales, where Frank was general manager.

Almost every type of vehicle in the General Motors lineup was sold at Smith Motor Sales. Reflections of potted plants and gleaming Cadillacs, Buicks, LaSalles, Oldsmobiles, Pontiacs, and GMC trucks shimmered in the waxed floors of the bright and airy showroom, and Frank could spot browsers from within his glass-walled office. Frank was the smiling face, the welcoming handshake, and the full embodiment of the family-oriented business mentality that defined Smith Motor Sales.

By spending time at Smith Motor Sales after school, Dave was able to see a side of his father he otherwise would not have glimpsed, and he picked up some tips on how to treat people from watching his father in action. One day, for instance, his father came out of his office to greet a gentleman who was meandering around the showroom with his hands in his pockets, peeking inside the cars on display.

"Joe," Frank said, extending his hand, "what are you doing here? It's not time for you to buy a new car."

"Well, Frank, my car is back in the shop. I'm just killing time while it's being repaired."

"Why didn't you tell me that your car was in for service?"

"I wouldn't do that—I don't want to bother you."

Protesting that helping him was never a bother, Frank steered his customer toward the service shop.

"Come on," he said. "Let's check on what's happening with your car."

Curious, Dave followed. He watched as his father introduced his customer to the service foreman, who reassured both Frank and Joe that the mechanic who had been assigned to do the repairs was experienced, conscientious, and skilled. Frank asked his foreman to watch over the repairs and thanked him for his time.

Dave trailed behind as his father escorted his customer to the parking lot. Pausing beside a burgundy Buick, Frank pulled a key ring from his pocket.

"Here, Joe. Take my car. You should not have to waste any more of your time. We'll call you when your car is ready."

Another day, Dave was at the dealership when a General Motors regional representative stopped in. He showed Frank a neon sign that read POWER STEERING.

"We'd like for you to have this," said the sales rep.

"Well, thank you," said Frank. "How much is it?"

"Two hundred dollars."

Dave knew that this garish sign was not the type of thing his father featured in his showroom. Yet Frank bought it. After the rep left, Frank asked his son to take the neon sign to the back room and put it in the bin where used items were made available to anyone in the shop who might want them. On their way home Dave asked his father why he had purchased the sign.

"What we must understand, son, is that this man may have a salary, but that selling something extra like this allows him to earn a bonus from the company."

When a union representative came in and tried to unionize Smith Motor Sales workers, Frank's advice to the employees was to go right ahead if that was what they wanted. None were interested. They knew that if they had a problem they could take it up with Frank Link.

Frank treated suppliers, customers, and employees as if they were members of an extended family, and Dave would incorporate this approach in his own careers. So Dave was ushered to the threshold of adulthood by a man who was an excellent role model as well as a loving, constant presence.

Dave later looked back on his childhood and decided that the most enduring gift he had received from his father was the love and respect that Frank had showered on Amelia. For example, every evening when it was time to go home, Frank telephoned Amelia from his office and asked what she would like him to pick up from the grocer. Father and son would stop at the store and buy whatever Amelia needed to complete dinner. When the two of them came through the door, Amelia was there to greet them with a kiss. Frank handed his wife the grocer-wrapped package, which she took into the kitchen. After spending a few minutes putting their dinner on the stove to simmer, or in the oven to bake, Amelia joined her husband in the living room where they shared the news of the day. Young Dave often popped into the living room before tackling his homework to let his folks know about the upcoming events at St. Mary's High School. For Dave, there was always lots to talk about. Among other extracurricular activities, Dave was a varsity player on three teams, a coeditor in chief of the school newspaper, and the writer of a sports column, Off the Cuff, which was published under the byline "Cuff Link," after the nickname given to him by his teammates. Beginning in December of his senior year, Dave was very likely to have something to say to his parents during their evening conversations about his steady girl, Barbara Ann Winterhalter.

One day stands out as the beginning of Dave's lifelong infatuation with Barbara. He was in his junior year. Barb, a sophomore, had landed the role of Mary, the mother of Jesus, in a school play. As Dave sat in the audience and watched Barbara on stage, there was something about the sound of her voice as she spoke her lines, something about the way she looked as the spotlight shone upon her cheekbones that captured Dave's full attention. "This is a woman of *exquisite* beauty," he thought to himself.

Once they began to date and he started to get to know her, Barbara's wit and intelligence rendered him forever smitten. Dave loved all sports; Barb was a popular, vivacious cheerleader. Dave loved all kinds of books; Barb's reading list made him feel parochial. Dave was the life of the party; Barb's steady sweetness drew people to her. From senior year on, there was nobody but Barbara for Dave.

In August 1954 Dave entered the University of Notre Dame, the only school to which he had applied. He was drawn to Notre Dame by a lifelong love for the Fighting Irish and by his admiration for the university's president, Reverend Theodore Martin Hesburgh, CSC, STD, who was known the world over as

Father Ted. During his thirty-five years as president, thousands of young people were drawn to the campus because of Father Ted's magnetism.

Dave quickly discovered that this larger-than-life international leader was as down-to-earth as, well, a father. Each year, new students are welcomed into the Notre Dame family at the celebration of the freshman orientation Mass. In 1954 Dave was an altar server for this Mass, the principal celebrant of which was none other than the president. As Dave was donning his cassock and surplice, Father Ted walked into the sacristy and introduced himself to each of the servers. After meeting Dave, Father Ted asked, "Where are you from, son?"

"I'm from Sandusky, Ohio, Father."

"Oh, the City of Beautiful Parks! I've been there a number of times." Dave felt as though he had been honored.

In October of his sophomore year, the sudden death of his dad rocked Dave's world. Suddenly the hours they had spent together at the car dealership, at home after school, and talking with Amelia at the twilight hour acquired heightened significance. Though Dave would miss his father, he was grateful for the quality time they had shared. But from this terrible misfortune came one of Dave's most auspicious blessings: a surrogate father. Not long after Dave returned to Notre Dame he received a call from the president's office. Father Ted wanted to express his condolences, and he invited Dave to come and talk with him. The compassionate mentoring that Father Ted gave to Dave during this meeting and afterward, throughout his life, bridged the enormous chasm created by the death of Frank Link.

Father Ted explains why he stepped in to help. "When I was

president, I belonged to everybody. If people had special needs, like losing a father, I felt that I had a special care of them. I did what I could to 'parent,' if you will, those who were deprived of that kind of leadership."

For all four of his undergraduate years, Dave wrote a letter and mailed it off to Barbara each and every day. Sometimes he wrote twice a day. He laughed when he received some of those missives back with Barbara's red-inked grammatical corrections sprinkled over the pages.

He and Barbara were married on July 12, 1958, two months after Dave was awarded his degree. They had set off for their honeymoon when the naive bridegroom panicked: what if the hotel management would not let him register without proof that he and Barbara were married? Always respectful of the conventions of propriety, Dave turned the car around and went to fetch the marriage license.

In marrying Barbara, Dave set the stage for the rest of his life.

Each time a man stands up for an ideal or acts to improve the lot of others, or strikes out against injustice, he sends forth a tiny ripple of hope, and crossing each other from a million different centers of energy and daring, those ripples build a current which can sweep down the mightiest walls of oppression and resistance.

—Robert F. Kennedy, Day of Affirmation Address,
University of Cape Town, South Africa, June 6, 1966

2. STUDENT TEACHER

In the 1950s, Notre Dame Law School followed the British system of legal education. Under this system, midterm and final exams did not cover only the material for that particular course. Exams were viewed as opportunities to test overall knowledge in every aspect of the law all during the three-year course of study, so the exams were comprehensive from semester to semester and from year to year.

Despite his own grueling curriculum as a student at the Law School, Dave also taught undergraduate courses at the University of Notre Dame. He came to believe that this was the biggest professional break of his life.

"While I was a law student," he recalls, "I was very lucky to have a teaching fellowship. The small income was essential to Barbara and me. Without it I couldn't finish law school. One semester I was supposed to teach Business Law, but the chairman of the Business Administration Department called me after registration and told me that enrollment was light and the course would not be offered. We hung up. I felt sick to my stomach. What was I going to do? And how could I break the news to Barbara?"

The chairman called back fifteen minutes later. He asked if Dave remembered enough accounting to be able to teach Accounting I to undergraduates.

"Sir, I will teach Greek mythology for the money."

The chairman chuckled. "Well, Dave, you don't have to teach Greek mythology, but if you can teach basic accounting, we'll switch you to Business Law later on."

So Dave taught Accounting I.

"Teaching accounting to undergraduates made me realize that I could learn more about any given subject by teaching it than I could by studying it. I would take the students' questions out of the classroom, think about them, and research them. I came away more informed than ever before. Fifteen years later, when I came to teach as a professor at the Law School, this lesson was still fresh in my mind, that I was going to learn even more about Federal Taxation, or Corporate Taxation, or whatever it was I was teaching, than I had learned when I was a student."

He must have done an adequate job with Accounting I since he was asked to add Accounting II to his teaching schedule, and he was happy to accept the offer.

Home for the newlyweds was a small apartment in a community known as Vetville, which housed only married graduate students who were, or were about to become, parents. The rent was unbeatable at $33 a month. Dave and Barb were blessed with two children during these law school years. David Christopher was born on August 6, 1959, Mary Teresa on St. Patrick's Day in 1961. Vetville neighbors became lifelong friends. Two in particular, Thomas L. "Tom" and Nancy Shaffer, would have a seminal influence on the course of Dave and Barb's lives.

Dave was awarded his Juris Doctor in May 1961. He was told that he had placed second in the state of Ohio on the bar examination. He launched his professional career by accepting a position as trial attorney in the United States Treasury (Internal Revenue Service) in the Office of Chief Counsel in Washington, D.C. He and Barbara and their two children moved to Arlington, Virginia.

Reporting to the office on his first day of work, Dave learned that his supervising boss, division director Christopher J. "Chris" Ray, nurtured an abiding and unconditional love for all sports and was overjoyed to have a Notre Dame alumnus on his staff. At long last, he enthused, he would be able to talk sports with a Domer. Dave learned to study up and be prepared. Every night, in order to keep up with new Federal regulations and learn how significant cases had been decided, Dave read the advance sheets in the field of Federal Taxation. Then, he combed the sports pages. Every morning he was called into Chris's office to rehash the developments of the previous day in the world of sports. The ritual helped foster a close working relationship between the two men.

Within one month of beginning his work at Treasury, Dave was inspired by President John F. Kennedy's idealism to serve his country by joining the Naval Reserves. Talking it over with Barbara, Dave said, "I just think I need to do this."

"You'll have to be gone."

"Yes. I know that. But I feel as though I have a patriotic duty to do this."

"Well, if you think that's what you ought to do," she said, "then that's what you ought to do."

When Dave informed his boss that he had joined the Naval Reserves, a move that would interrupt his work at Treasury, Chris's response was, "That's great. Now, have you had a chance to look at today's sports pages?"

After hearing through the department grapevine that Dave could do a spot-on imitation of President Kennedy, Chris called him into his office one day. He explained that the department had a long-standing tradition of putting on a comedy skit at the annual departmental Christmas party. Crane Hauser, who had recently been appointed chief counsel of the Internal Revenue Service and assistant general counsel of the Treasury Department by his friend President Kennedy, would be at the party.

"Now, Dave," said Chris, "I understand you do a pretty good impersonation of President Kennedy. Since the new chief counsel will be at the Christmas party, I want you to do your impression in the skit."

"I can't do that," Dave protested. "I don't know what kind of sense of humor this guy has!"

"I can assure you that he has a good sense of humor, Dave. Plan on doing your impersonation at the party."

Dave did as he was told, the new chief counsel was indeed a good sport about Dave's impersonation of the president, and it seemed as though that was the end of the matter.

In the first weeks of 1962, however, Chief Counsel Hauser set about naming members to his prestigious new Special Advisory Committee. One problem the Special Advisory Committee would be charged with solving was the enormous number of conflicts that were arising in Internal Revenue offices all across the country. The chief counsel was set on eliminating the many regional inconsistencies in how cases were being handled. He also was determined to create a standardized system for how those cases were being written up.

As relayed to Dave by Chris, Chief Hauser had been urged by an advisor to select at least one young professional to serve on the otherwise white-haired committee. The chief counsel had responded that he liked the idea but there was a problem: he didn't *know* any of the young people. Almost as soon as the words were out of his mouth, Chief Hauser interrupted his own protestation, saying, "Hey, wait a minute—what about the kid who did the Kennedy impersonation at the Christmas party?" So Dave was recruited to serve on the Special Advisory Committee with this very senior, very elite group.

As Dave and Chris made their way to the first official meeting, Chris gave Dave sage advice about the comportment that was appropriate for the committee's token youngster.

"Look here, Dave. You're going to be the youngest guy by far in this group. What you should do is just sit there and listen. Whatever you do, don't ask any questions. We'll go somewhere afterward and talk about everything."

Dave and Chris entered a majestic conference room that was exquisitely appointed all the way down to white wall-to-wall carpeting. After all the members had settled themselves around a mahogany table, Chief Hauser rose from his seat at the head of the table to deliver his opening remarks.

Dave pulled a pipe from his suit coat pocket and began the ritualistic tamping down of tobacco. He struck a match to light the pipe but neglected to close the cover. Sparks ignited the entire matchbook and suddenly he was holding a conflagration in his hand. When it singed his fingers, he reflexively tossed the matchbook into the air. The fireball fell to the floor. Dave leaped to his feet so that he could stomp out the flames.

After picking up the smoldering matchbook, Dave stood for a moment considering whether there would be a wastebasket in such a pristine room. Meanwhile, silence assaulted him from every side.

Chris saved the day for the kid whose Kennedy impersonation couldn't help him now. He said, "Dave, next time you have a question, why don't you just raise your hand?"

The committee decided that a computerized system was the answer to Chief Hauser's challenge. A brilliant systems analyst named Al Alowine was hired to write a program that would enable the IRS to track cases throughout all its offices. When it came to computer design, no one could top Al. However, not knowing anything about taxation or the law, Al could not make much progress on the project. The obvious solution was to train a tax attorney in computers and then pair him up with Al.

The chief counsel chose Dave and named him chief of Reports and Information Retrieval Activity (RIRA). This was a significant position. Being a branch chief with supervisory status entitled Dave to attend a special symposium, the brainchild of Attorney General Robert F. "Bobby" Kennedy.

The attorney general had lined up a slate of presentations to be made by some of the most influential men of the times, all of whom were African Americans. The overarching theme of the conference was the need for integration in government supervisory positions. Attendance was by invitation only. Dave was one of about 150 supervisors who gathered in an auditorium in the Commerce Building for the presentations.

Bobby Kennedy launched the series with a welcoming address in which he issued a clarion call for change. Dave recalls that the attorney general instructed everyone to "look around this room. Everyone in this auditorium is in a supervisory position. Notice that almost all of you are white males. We have to do something about that. We must figure out ways to get more women and minorities into supervisory positions. I am presenting a series of speakers who will talk to us about just how important it is for us to get this done."

From that day forward, Bobby Kennedy was on Dave Link's short list of real-life heroes. Dave couldn't wait to recap the meeting for Barbara. "Bobby doesn't pull any punches, Barbara," he told his wife. "He is talking about how 'this is not what we *ought* to do.' He says that 'this is what we *have* to do.' This goes beyond the Justice Department, Barb. This is huge."

All of the speeches in the symposium were eye-opening, but as far as Dave was concerned the most riveting speaker was Dr. Martin Luther King Jr., who spoke about the morality of a social conscience, and about the critical imperative to bring about a change in the public's perception of minorities. Dr. King's speech flipped a switch inside Dave's mind. He came away with a new perception of the world and the role that he could play in it.

Dave and Barb sat up late at night discussing the ideas that had been fleshed out in Kennedy's symposium, ideas such as social justice is something that must be implemented in everything that we do. They looked around and were shocked to discover that there was great opposition to court-ordered school desegregation where they lived, in Arlington County. They felt that this was a compelling reason to get involved in their community. They decided to lend their efforts to the local grassroots civil rights movement. It was a decision that gave birth to an identity that would stick throughout their marriage. Dave and Barb became a couple who always found time to work for justice in addition to meeting the demands of church, family, and career.

One way in which they became activists was by becoming involved with the Northern Virginia Human Relations Commission. In those days the membership roster was limited to men only, but Barbara was, as always, Dave's enthusiastic partner in the endeavor. The commission had been formed, in part, to help implement court-ordered integration of Northern Virginia's schools. It took courage to belong to this group. The head of the American Nazi Party, George Lincoln Rockwell, lived within their jurisdiction, and members of his party would sic dogs on commission workers as they campaigned. As if that was not daunting enough, commission workers were also confronted by police who threatened to arrest them if they did not agree to stop going door-to-door. Dave and his co-campaigners seemed to be encountering resistance from all sides.

Dave and Barbara also joined the ABC, or Arlingtonians for a Better County, political party. Running on an earnest platform that promised *We can do a better job,* volunteers went door-to-door in the hopes of opening up a dialogue about desegregation and civil rights. The members of ABC were successful in electing a new county board that was, in turn, victorious in implementing desegregation throughout Arlington County's schools.

But it was a tough campaign. Just as with the Northern Virginia Human Relations Commission, ABC volunteers endured harassment. Anti-ABC goons roamed the streets and attempted to intimidate the volunteers into abandoning their work. Dave remembers visiting one home in particular. His knock had been answered by a preteen.

Through his work and volunteer activities, Dave had become a visible member of the community. At Blessed Sacrament Catholic School in Alexandria, for example, Dave coached seventh- and eighth-grade boys basketball, seventh- and eighth-grade girls basketball and softball, and served the school as athletic director and the church as head of the parish council.

So it was disappointing that as he and the student stood on either side of the partially opened door, Dave heard the voice of a woman shouting, "Slam the door! That man is in favor of black people—and besides, he's *Catholic!*"

In the meantime, Dave entered the Navy Reserves as a Judge Advocate General (JAG) officer. The first time he was called into active duty he was sent to the Naval Justice School in Newport, Rhode Island, where he completed six weeks of training in military law. Since graduation from the Naval Justice School is rewarded with a promotion, Dave would depart with the rank of lieutenant. Just a few days after he arrived at the school, an admiral's aide approached the table at which Dave and others were seated for lunch.

"Are you Link?"

"Yes, sir, I am."

"The admiral wants you to sit at his table for lunch."

"I'm a lieutenant junior grade!"

"Let me repeat. The admiral wants you to sit at his table for lunch."

Dave joined the admiral at his table for lunch.

The admiral wasted no time in presenting his agenda.

"Son," he began, "I understand you know something about computers."

"Yes, sir, I do," replied Dave.

"Well, we have plenty of lawyers in this outfit. But very few of us know anything about computers. More importantly, we don't have anybody here who can teach us about computers. I want you to teach a course on computers."

"I'm a student here, sir."

"I'm an admiral here, and I can do anything I want. You will continue being a student. You will learn all that we need to teach you about the navy. But you will also teach us about computers."

Once again, just as in law school, Dave was both student and teacher.

For another tour of duty, Dave was called from his work at the Treasury for a week during which the strength of his convictions would be put to the test. The general counsel for the navy had resigned, and the new appointee would not be able to assume the position until the following week. At twenty-six years of age, Dave became the acting general counsel of the United States Navy.

One day during that week, a navy captain came into Dave's office to ask that Dave give him a letter stating that the monetary award he had won for a naval invention was a tax-free prize.

"I would like to do that for you, sir," Dave replied. "But I can't. This prize is not tax-free."

The captain shot back, "Of course it is. Section 71 of the Internal Revenue Code says that it's tax-free."

"No, sir. Section 71 says that the only prizes that are tax-free are prizes such as the Nobel Peace Prize. The award that you received from the navy is in connection with your work, so it is a bonus, not a prize."

"Well, I think it's a tax-free prize, and all I need is a letter from you."

"Sir, it is not a tax-free prize. I cannot give you that letter."

The captain glowered at the kid on the other side of the desk. "How many stripes are on your sleeve?"

"Two, sir," Dave replied.

"How many are on my sleeve?"

"Four, sir."

"Does that mean that I outrank you?"

"Yes, sir, it does."

"I am now ordering you to give me that letter."

"You can't do that, sir. You cannot order me to do something that is illegal."

The captain stormed from the office after raging that Dave

would be receiving orders from the admiral that he was to write the letter. Dave brought the matter to the attention of the admiral, who shook his head. The captain had been out of line, he said, adding, "I would never order you or anyone else to do anything that was illegal."

During his time in D.C., Dave was an avid participant in interoffice sports. In the fall of 1962 the flag football team on which Dave played did well enough to make it all the way to the finals. The title of champions would be decided in a contest between the Justice Department and the Department of Labor in a game that was to be played on the White House lawn.

Famously unable to resist a pickup game of any kind, President Kennedy took a break from his work to step outside the Oval Office and watch some of the action. The players paused, awed at the sight of their president standing with his arms crossed, smiling. Chills went up and down Dave's entire being.

When the men resumed the game, they dug in and played with a ferocity born of the desire to impress the commander in chief. The president stood there for a while longer, looking wistful, as if what he really wanted to do was forget for just a few moments that he was president and join in the fun.

On Friday, November 22, Dave and Al Alowine spent the morning at the United States Navy's Maryland Computer Center inputting adjustments to the program they had written for the navy's state-of-the-art punch-card-operated IBM 1410 computer, which employed the FORTRAN programming language.

They drove to a local restaurant for lunch. When they stepped inside they knew in an instant that something was wrong. A large crowd was clustered in a semicircle around the polished oaken bar. All eyes were fixed on a radio that blared from a shelf amidst the liquor bottles. Dave and Al leaned in to hear the broadcaster announce that President Kennedy had been shot. They raced back out to the car, jumped in, and made a beeline for the nation's capital.

President Kennedy's assassination had a profound effect on Dave's life. "I prayed. And I cried. I thought about how the world would change without Jack. And, of course, it did."

Never again would Dave perform his imitation of President Kennedy. Dave decided that this would be his way of giving tribute and thanks to the Kennedy brothers for their magnificent influence in shaping his life.

The second and final time Dave was near the president was on November 25, 1963, the day that Jack Kennedy was laid to rest in Arlington Cemetery.

Dave had gone to the office expecting to work. Once there, he was too distracted to concentrate. Early in the afternoon, responding to something that felt like a calling, he put on his overcoat, went down the elevator to the first floor, and exited the Internal Revenue Service Building. His footsteps led him up Constitution Avenue and across Henry Bacon Drive to Lincoln Memorial Circle. He was roused from a fog of reverie as he passed beneath the downcast eyes of the president who had borne the weight of the Civil War on his shoulders. Dave stopped, looked up at the magnificent statue, and was shaken by worries of what the future might hold for the country. Was America destined to suffer like it had after President Lincoln's assassination? He turned toward the Arlington Memorial Bridge and walked on, all the while praying for America.

He entered Arlington National Cemetery through the Memorial Gate. Drawn by an unknown force to a particular spot, he found himself in a grove of trees just a few feet from the burial vault. It felt as if not much time elapsed before he heard the lonely drum cadence, and then the clippity-clop of horse hooves as six matched grays pulled a creaking wooden caisson up the rise where they halted, finally, on a gentle slope just east of the Custis-Lee Mansion.

The odd stillness was broken by the Marine band, which opened the burial service with the playing of the most haunting rendition of the national anthem Dave had ever heard. He watched as the Kennedy family members and dignitaries were escorted from their limousines to the grave site. The U.S. Air Force bagpipe band began a slow march from the far side of the grave, crossing right in front of Dave as pipers played a lament, "Mist Covered Mountain," that resounded throughout the cemetery.

As the last of the bagpipe tones were absorbed into the hills, the air was suddenly shattered with the roar of a thunderous flyover. Fifty fighter aircraft—one for each state in the union— streaked by, low and ferocious, in three V formations. One plane was missing from the third configuration, a tribute to the fallen commander in chief.

In that moment, Dave made a vow: *I have to do something worthwhile with my life.*

Life's most persistent and urgent question is "What are you doing for others?" —The Reverend Martin Luther King Jr.

3. CHICAGO

Dave and Barb were happy in Arlington. The family had grown with the birth of Maureen Elizabeth on August 25, 1962. The Links had made wonderful friends, and they were flourishing in their civil rights work.

In 1964 Dave became the first person to receive both the Younger Federal Lawyer Award and the Secretary of the Treasury Certificate for Outstanding Service to the United States, two of the highest honors an attorney could receive from the federal government. Dave interpreted this unprecedented achievement as a sign that it was time for him to think about moving on. This established a pattern that Dave would follow throughout his life: after having reached some pinnacle of achievement, Dave would be filled with a sense of restiveness and would pick up the banner of a new cause.

Dave began the process of interviewing at law firms. He would make a selection based on a work philosophy to which both he and Barb were committed. They agreed that an essential component of every legal practice is pro bono work, which is work that an attorney does for people who cannot afford legal representation. Dave and Barb viewed this kind of public service as both the responsibility and the privilege of every attorney-at-law.

When Dave interviewed at prestigious Winston, Strawn, Smith and Patterson in Chicago, he made a proposal. He promised that he would set a firm-wide record for billable hours. In return, he asked that he be permitted to utilize all of the firm's facilities in representing the poor for free every Thursday. The firm accepted Dave's proposal. In 1965 Dave was appointed a senior associate attorney at Winston, Strawn. The family pulled up stakes and returned to the Midwest.

They moved to Wilmette, Illinois, a community fourteen miles north of Chicago. Dave commuted by train to the firm's downtown Chicago offices. His specialty, international and federal tax law, ensured that he would represent clients who had complex and interesting problems, and he loved what he was doing. After the first year, in which he did, as promised, set a firm-wide record for billable hours, Dave was promoted to partner. Two years later, in 1968, Dave was promoted to senior partner. For Dave, however, the best part of the work he was doing at his firm was his "Thursday Practice." This pro bono work prefigured the future by leading Dave into communities he otherwise would not have known existed.

Dave's journey into unfamiliar territory began when members of the Chicago Bar Association contacted him to ask for his help in fighting a regulation that Chicago Realtors had been successful in getting passed. The regulation was despicable in a way that was not unlike the sharecropping system of the Reconstruction era in the South. Just as some white former slave owners took advantage of uneducated freedmen, some Chicago Realtors were taking advantage of people who were too poor to afford a down payment, as well as immigrants who were not fluent in speaking or reading English. These homebuyers were being presented with contracts that provided financiers the option of taking possession of the property in question if mortgage payments arrived after the due date. In the beginning years of the contract, if the homeowners were in fact late with a payment, the mortgage lenders reassured them that the late payment was not of consequence. Thus the homeowners were lulled into thinking that tardiness per se was not a problem so long as the payments were made in due course. Yet the finance companies would use late payments as an excuse for foreclosing on properties when the homeowners got to the final few months of their contracts. After having paid on a house for many years, people suddenly found themselves evicted due to the enforcement of a late payment clause that had been waived throughout the previous years.

A team of crusaders assembled to put an end to this reprehensible scheme. A class action lawsuit was filed on behalf of hundreds of clients. Six attorneys participated in developing and litigating the case. Each was associated with a different high-powered firm, and each devoted two and a half years of pro bono work to the case. Dave was one of the six.

As the public-information guy on the team, Dave's responsibilities included speaking with Mayor Richard J. Daley's staff, the press, media, and groups of clients and concerned citizens who gathered for meetings in churches and schools all around Chicago. Attorney Dave Link was welcomed into neighborhoods that are normally off-limits to white-collar professionals. One night, for example, Dave was scheduled to explain developments in the case to a group of clients, and the designated meeting place was a church located in the heart of Blackstone Ranger territory on the southwest side of Chicago.

The Blackstone Rangers had evolved from a community organization in the late 1950s to the most powerful and dangerous Chicago gang in the 1960s. When Dave was given the address where the meeting was to be held, one of the other lawyers on the team reassured him that the Blackstone Rangers were appreciative of the work the team of lawyers was doing on what had become known as the Contract Buyers League case.

Dave set out from home in the family car. He drove past the University of Chicago along South Parkway, now Martin Luther King Drive. When he entered Woodlawn, his progress was halted by a uniformed Blackstone Ranger who stepped to the middle of the road, arm extended and palm turned toward him in the classic traffic-cop gesture. Dave rolled down his window. The youth checked the photo that he was holding in his hand, saw that the image matched the face of the man before him, and leaned in.

"Mr. Link, we are proud to have you in our territory."

"Thank you. I'm proud to be here."

"Listen to these directions very carefully. As you proceed toward the church, you will be stopped at three more checkpoints. You will come to a Ranger whose job is to park your car for you. Just give him your keys. You will not have to worry about your car, Mr. Link; it will be protected. Another Ranger will escort you into the church, and he will stay at your side while you are here."

Dave was the only Caucasian in a church that was packed, standing room only, with concerned citizens. He gave a status report on the case and fielded questions, some of which necessitated the help of a translator. At the conclusion of the meeting, the Blackstone Rangers were standing by to ensure Dave's safe departure from Woodlawn with the same attention to detail they had exercised earlier that evening.

The attorneys took the case to trial and they won. The regulation was expunged. People got their houses back. One attorney on the team, a man who spoke fluent Spanish, followed up with a program designed to teach people how to protect themselves in the future from unfair practices like the contract buying scheme.

As a couple, Barb and Dave were simpatico, so much so that Dave was able to make important decisions or embark on a new path without having to consult Barbara first. Their like-mindedness was put to the test when the managing partner of Winston, Strawn called Dave into his office one day.

One of the firm's clients lived on the same street as the Link residence. He had called the firm, incensed. He said that he had seen an African American child going in and out of the Link house and playing outside with the Link children. It was inconceivable that the child was living with the Links, he said, yet it appeared as though that was the case.

Dave sat across from his boss and explained that little Carl Witherspoon was indeed living with the Links. Carl had come to them through a summer program that placed underprivileged children in loving homes. The children were treated to a couple of months away from the stress, heat, and environmental deprivation they would have experienced in Chicago's inner-city neighborhoods.

The managing partner explained to Dave that the firm's client considered Carl's living in his neighborhood to be an untenable situation. In fact, the client had threatened to pull all of his business from the firm if Dave did not "get rid of that kid." So, he said, Dave must send the child back.

Without hesitation Dave said, "Absolutely not."

"Even if it means your job, Dave?"

"I'll have another job by the end of the afternoon."

Now, Dave did not actually believe that he could pull off such a feat. Thinking fast, he made a counterproposal. He asked for the chance to speak with the client himself. Dave's boss agreed and placed a call to the client.

The client was quick to boast that he served on the board of directors of a local orphanage and sneered, "If you're such a do-gooder, Link, why don't you take in a kid from the orphanage?"

"That's a great idea," Dave replied. "Can you please give me a name? I would be happy to go out to the orphanage this afternoon and pick up any child you name."

There was silence at the other end of the telephone.

"Do you *know* the names of any of the orphans who live at the orphanage?"

Silence.

Finally, the client sputtered, "No. No, but . . . but I am on the board! I will get the address of the orphanage . . . and . . . and I can get a name . . . The people there will give me a name . . ."

Dave interjected, "I'll make you a deal. Just get me the name of a child, and I will go pick that child up and take him or her home with me. The child can stay with me and my family and Carl for the rest of the summer."

The client must have understood the point that Dave was making. Dave and his boss heard a click as the client slammed down his telephone.

Not long after, the client placed another call to the firm. As president of his company, he said, he would be pulling all of his business. As luck would have it, the matter ended well for Winston, Strawn. The client needed the approval of his company's chair of the board, who just happened to be his wife, and she refused to sever ties with the law firm that had served her father so well during all the years when he was building up the business that she had inherited.

When Dave told Barbara about the controversy over Carl's presence in their home and what his response had been, her eyes shone with pride. She uttered not one word about the frightening possibility of Dave losing his job.

When the Links moved into Wilmette, only two African Americans, a husband and wife, could be counted among the population of the village. The couple, however, did not own the property where they resided. They lived in the carriage house and worked as chauffeur and maid for the Caucasian homeowners. Dave and Barb were determined to help break down the racial divide in their community. To that end, they served as chair-couple of the North Shore Human Relations Committee, later renamed the Wilmette Human Relations Committee, the purpose of which was to help integrate Chicago's northern suburbs.

Their progressivism was rewarded with a slew of threatening phone calls that Barbara fielded at the Link residence. Among other things, Barbara was warned not to let her children walk to school. Dave didn't like that Barb and the children were being placed on the front line. He sat down and talked with Barb about the threats, but she brushed him off.

"I'm not worried," she told him.

"I don't want you to have to go through this, Barb. You're the one who has to answer these horrible phone calls."

"No, no," she insisted. "I'm with you on this, Dave."

She elaborated by saying, "You see, we have this blindness in society, and these people are simply blind in a particular way. But that doesn't mean that they aren't charitable people."

In the five years that the Links lived in Wilmette, they saw some progress in the reduction of racial prejudice. By the time they left Illinois for Indiana, census figures showed that there were four and a half black families living in Wilmette. The fact that a great deal remained to be done was made clear not only when some residents grumbled that Dave and Barb had been the ruination of their village, but even more so when the prevailing opinion singled out as the most incendiary of those four and a half families a biracial couple who had moved into the gorgeous white house across the street from the Baha'i Temple—the house that is reserved for the chairman of the temple and his wife and family.

D ave was having the time of his life at Winston, Strawn and was ecstatic to be promoted to senior partner at the age of thirty-two. When he told Barbara his news, he was surprised at her reaction. She shook her head and her mouth curved into a little smile.

"They shouldn't have done that," she murmured, as if talking to herself.

"What do you mean, Barb? This is great! This is all I've ever wanted!"

"We'll have moved on within a year."

She was right.

Barbara was proved correct when their friends from Vetville, Tom and Nancy Shaffer, came to Wilmette at the end of October 1969 and made Dave an offer he could not refuse.

In 1963, while Dave was working for the federal government, Tom had joined the faculty of Notre Dame Law School. In 1969 Tom was appointed associate dean. It was in this capacity that he came to Dave with a proposal.

The Links were still reeling from a great sadness when the Shaffers came to visit. Barb, Dave, and the children had been anticipating with excitement the birth of a new addition to the family when they learned that the baby had died in utero. Doctors suspected that Rh blood incompatibility was the cause of the baby's death. Barbara carried the baby to term knowing that her child would be stillborn, and on October 21, 1969, she endured labor and delivery.

Barb and Dave named their new daughter Little Barbara and made plans to bury her in a cemetery in Des Plaines.

The parents grieved quietly. There were no histrionics. No outbursts. Just a heavy air of reverence for a loss that was too great to be understood; it could only be accepted. David Christopher, Mary, and Maureen would remember the tiny white casket and the sad but sweet expression on their mother's face as she explained that it was God's will that their baby sister go straight to heaven.

Tom and Nancy arrived in Wilmette within two weeks of Little Barbara's burial. Tom and Dave slipped away for lunch, and Tom took the opportunity to pitch a life-altering idea to his friend. The tax law professor who had taught both Dave and Tom was retiring, he explained. He wanted Dave to replace the departing professor and invited Dave to join the faculty of Notre Dame Law School.

It was a career change that would mean a significant reduction in Dave's earnings as well as a radical refocusing of his legal career. Even so, Dave heard a call he was compelled to answer.

Years later Tom chuckled as he remembered how long it took Dave to make up his mind. "Dave told me he would think about it. But he didn't think long. He's quick at knowing an open door that he wants to go through."

That very night Dave and Barb agreed that they would go home. Home to Notre Dame.

PART TWO

COMMUNITY

If the stars should appear but one night every thousand years how man would believe and adore. —Ralph Waldo Emerson

Ralph Waldo Emerson once asked what we would do if the stars only came out once every thousand years. No one would sleep that night, of course. The world would create new religions overnight. We would be ecstatic, delirious, made rapturous by the glory of God. Instead, the stars come out every night, and we watch television.

—Paul Hawken, from his commencement address to the Class of 2009, University of Portland (Oregon), May 3, 2009

Prison as Community

As communities, prisons are mirrors. Microcosms of the macrocosm. The trick to understanding the American prison empire is to realize that crime is not driving the engine of incarceration. Prisons are at the caboose end of a runaway train that is tugging boxcar after boxcar filled with economic disenfranchisement, fear, inertia, legislative Jim Crowism, and unresolved prejudices. Prisons reflect the society in which they are embedded.

Before he started teaching at the prison, Dave saw criminals as indistinctly as if they were extras in grainy silent movies. As he spent time at Indiana State Prison, one by one the men at the prison brought Technicolor to Dave's concept of criminality, and

Dave's perception was changed. He no longer looked at the men and saw a prison population. He saw a population of individuals who were prisoners.

As a new volunteer at Indiana State Prison, Dave was inexperienced but open-minded. He jumped onto a learning curve and followed it all across the prison complex. He learned that most prisoners had been living purposeless lives before their incarceration and that being in prison has the effect of implanting in them the belief that their lives are without value. He learned that programs designed to habilitate inmates suffer from the too little, too late syndrome. ("To say 'rehabilitate' suggests that these men had a chance in the first place," he would tell people on the outside.) He was astounded at the idiocy of drug treatment programs; for instance, enrollment in the narcotics program is made available not when people first enter the prison system but when they are within two years of release. Thus, people spend years in prison battling addictions without the benefit of counseling or treatment, wasting the opportunity they could have had to use their time in prison to work on sobriety and self-awareness.

The more often he went to Indiana State Prison, the more Dave realized that there was an untapped potential to transform lives behind The Wall. The men want to learn, but there aren't enough programs. There is no question, for example, that yoga classes are transformative, yet far too few men can take advantage of them because the demand exceeds the availability. The majority of prisoners are never exposed to the healing power inherent in the practice of meditation, nor to techniques that will help them replace anger, negative mind chatter, and circular thought patterns with empathy and compassion.

Before beginning work in the prison, Dave completed a week of orientation and jujitsu training for physical protection. Volunteers are granted two different levels of visitation privileges. Wearing a yellow badge is a signal to correctional officers that a volunteer can be inside the chapel. Wearing a blue badge signals that a volunteer is able to go anywhere inside the prison complex unaccompanied by staff. After being awarded a blue badge, Dave wasted no time in taking advantage of his visitation privileges. He roamed everywhere to learn the lay of the land and to introduce himself to correctional staff and prisoners alike. He became as knowledgeable about the prison as he was about his law school.

He learned that the residents of the housing units are sometimes in "lockdown" as punishment for an infringement committed by one of the residents. During lockdown men are unable to go anywhere—to the dining hall, to religious worship services, or to their jobs. Sack lunches consisting of four pieces of bread, one piece of cheese, an apple, and a cookie are delivered to their cells.

He learned that shivs are crude weapons made from taping two razor blades to a toilet paper tube. The more valuable prison commodity is the knife-like shank; some are crafted by filing locker door rods to a sharp point. One day a prisoner came racing into the chapel with another man fast on his heels. There had been an argument between the two. Weapons had been pulled, but the first man took off for the chapel. He knew that he would be protected by the unspoken rule that no act of violence will be allowed to defile the sanctuary. Once the men touched this sacred ground, the feud was over. The two sauntered out as if the fight had never happened.

Just as high schools use a system of bells to direct the movements of students between classes, a series of seven daily head counts control the activity and whereabouts of the men. The men are awakened at the first head count at 3:00 A.M., a ridiculously early hour that skews the entire day. Breakfast is available in the prisoners' dining hall starting at 3:30, but rather than avail themselves of breakfast, most of the guys opt for catching a little more sleep. The second head count is at 5:30, after which prisoners who have jobs are permitted to report for work. Following the 10:00 count, men are sent to the dining hall in three different shifts for lunch. Those who have jobs resume their work until the 2:00 P.M. count. Dinner follows close on the heels of this midafternoon count since a count at 5:30 marks the end of the prisoners' day. With few exceptions, prisoners are confined to their living quarters from the 5:30 count until the following morning. Two nighttime counts at 9:00 P.M. and midnight complete the correctional staff's cycle of keeping track of where each and every prisoner is at any given time. Once the men are released back into society, adjusting to a daily routine that does not begin at 3:30 in the morning is always tough.

When he was not teaching a class, Dave went from cell to cell and simply spent time with people. Prisoners began to confide in him. One of the first was Jason Garver.

Jason's hazel eyes peer out from oversized square eyeglass frames that would have been in fashion when he entered Indiana State Prison twenty-five years ago. He seems earnest but also shy and out of place. He moves quickly and efficiently, as if he is worried about getting in someone's way.

"When I first met him," Jason recalls, "Doc came in as a volunteer. He was a caring, loving guy. He opened my eyes up about God. He made me realize the crime I have done, but that God still loves me and forgives me. I was thinking about not being the altar person any more—too much politics—but he said leave the politics out of it and let the Lord take care of it. It was good advice. I looked forward to seeing him then, and I look forward to seeing him now. Sometimes when he doesn't come in, it breaks me down a little bit."

There are three predominant strategies for surviving behind The Wall. People endure by performing sexual favors, by joining a gang, or by keeping to themselves. Dave became knowledgeable about the prison subculture, where gangs, brutality, and cold-blooded narcissism are common. He attended a program in which lifers talked straight with high school teens. One of the students asked, "If a good friend of yours is stabbed, would you stop to help him?" The answer the student received was "Not on your life. If I stop to help him, I'm the next victim. The Good Samaritan rule may work on the outside. But in here, if my best friend were lying in a pool of blood, I'd just step over him."

It is not uncommon for prisoners to barge into an unlocked cell and threaten the occupant in some way, or steal from him, or rape him. The victim is fearful of making a report to the guards, as doing so might incur a punishment for the entire unit, in which case the other prisoners in his cell house would make certain that he would suffer further consequences for having ratted.

Tattoos are an important part of prison life. They help to project a tough image, they broadcast a person's identification with a gang, and they communicate subtle messages or warnings to other prisoners. Some men have teardrops tattooed on their cheeks, one for every person they have murdered. Of course, tattooing is prohibited by the prison administration. Even so, every prison has its tattoo artists. If any man is caught with inking equipment in his cell, he will be moved to an isolation unit. Hence tattoos are administered with the very crudest equipment, and infections are commonplace.

In prison, commissary is a big deal. Commissary offers men a chance to purchase snacks and the kind of junk food that is found in vending machines. Guys order what they want to buy from commissary one week in advance. Sometimes these treats can become bones of contention, prizes sought by prisoners who become like bounty hunters intimidating or threatening other prisoners to take possession of their snacks, or even stealing somebody else's commissary.

There were some prisoners Dave found difficult to be around. He discovered that in the prison community there are several kinds of predators—commissary predators, sexual predators, men who torment weaker prisoners, and bullies who are nothing more than thieves among thieves. He met men who had been manipulating other people all their lives. His background as a lawyer helped him spot the two hallmarks of manipulation: inconsistencies and contradictions. So when different prisoners told him multiple versions of a single incident that bore no resemblance to one another, Dave shut down the self-promotion. "Don't give me that garbage," he would say. The prisoners corrected their stories rather than risk losing his respect.

He met a lot of haters who made no secret of prejudices against people of another race, religion, background, or criminal history, as, for example, when prisoners made it their business to torment child molesters. Dave's strategy was to try to break these haters away from a universal mode of thinking. He used his litigation experience to lead them through a deposition-like line of questioning, asking, "Do you really believe that? Why do you believe that? Is this your experience with all people of this race/religion/ethnicity?" He then worked with the hater to identify and consider others in this particular target group who are good people, and this might lead to discussions about how there are good attributes in everyone, even people you do not like. Sometimes Dave shared his knowledge about specific individuals in the group that was being targeted by the hater. If the hater was intractable, Dave separated himself from the hatred by stating his disagreement with and refusal to sign on to the generalized opinion.

Yet prison life, ugly though it may be, can be punctuated by moments of grace that percolate up from deep within the cesspool.

Norman Blakely describes just such a moment.

"Doc became like a father to me. I could talk about any of my problems with him. The advice he gave me didn't come from an average man. He speaks a lot of love.

"One time he asked me to pray for a bad situation I was in. I took his advice, as though he really is my father. I prayed for the inmates as well as for staff members, and somehow it worked out that we have peace. Peace between me and that other inmate and peace between me and the staff. All because he asked me to pray for them. God works through this man. I feel it in my spirit for real."

Just like any community, Indiana State Prison has a distinct topography. Main Street runs about a quarter of a mile and stretches from the vegetable gardens through the outdoor recreation yards. A small red firehouse on Main Street has the quaint look of yesteryear. The firefighters who respond to alarms are prisoners. In addition to his responsibilities as a chapel musician, Bill Dixon also works as a fireman. When an alarm is sounded, correctional officers follow a set of procedures to release Bill and the rest of the fire department from wherever they may be so that they can tend to the emergency.

Some of the prisoners are landscapers who keep the grounds neat and trim. In the spring, Dave noticed perennials sprouting like random exclamation marks amidst the iron bars and crumbling facades of old buildings. Daffodils stood at attention at the base of a stone birdbath, and although Dave passed the birdbath many times, he never did see any birds taking advantage of the facilities.

Dave explored all the buildings that dot the campus. He checked out the site where the laundry is done for both the institution and the prisoners. He visited the hospital, a building just under a thousand square feet that was constructed in 1943. He poked around in the kitchen and explored the prisoners' dining hall, which consists of two expansive, open rooms filled with tables and chairs. The men arrive for meals in three different shifts. They choose from a regular line or a vegan line, and they have ten minutes in which to eat their meals. It is not surprising that obesity is a problem, because the prison diet is heavy on starches, with beans, cheese, mashed potatoes, bread, and cookies repeat-offenders among the cafeteria's offerings. Meats are usually some form of processed turkey. One night the guys were excited. They told Dave that they would be having "rolled steak" and urged him to come to dinner that night. He joined them inside the dining room, where several men jockeyed for the privilege of fetching his dinner. When the tray was placed before him, Dave was amused to find that his rolled steak was a hot dog.

The courses that Dave taught were held in one of two locations. Larger classes met inside the chapel; smaller classes were held inside a room in either of the two education buildings. One is known as Backstreet Education. This is the building in which the general library is housed. Dave donated two thousand volumes from his personal collection to this library. On the first floor of the other education building there is a law library, which is required by the Constitution. The second floor is dedicated to classroom space; the floors above are prison cells.

In one of Dave's classes he gave a lecture that teased out the differences between *wants* and *needs*. Afterward he passed out blank sheets of paper. He told his students that they were not to sign their names, and he hoped everyone would feel safe enough to share their innermost thoughts. They were to write down what they needed, really needed, in contrast to what they wanted. Dave collected the work at the end of class, took the sheaf of papers home, and ensconced himself in the living room on a blue velveteen upholstered chair to read them.

Some of his students had written of biological and physiological issues that speak to basic human needs. They wrote of needing a piece of good meat or a bowl of fresh strawberries. They wrote about needing sleep that was uninterrupted or just a little less uncomfortable.

Other students wrote of their need to feel safe and the need to escape the stress of living in a prison subculture of violence, gangs, and rivalries.

Many wrote about their wives and children and their need to see them, talk to them, and put their arms around them. Some men expressed a need to be connected to something on the outside. Many longed for visitors or for pen pals.

A few students wrote about needing a job or art supplies, or needing something meaningful to do with their time. One man's slanting scrawl covered all of the front side of the page and half of the back. He wrote of needing to be enrolled in school. He wanted to earn a degree, and what he needed more than anything else in the world was to learn.

Dave laid this answer on the stack of papers to his right. He picked up the next sheet from the pile to his left. Six words were enshrouded on the page.

I need to see the moon.

Dave took off his reading glasses, set them on the side table, and rose from his chair. As if in a trance, he wandered through the living and dining rooms to the back door, pushed open the screen, and stepped outside. He walked the entire length of the cedar balcony that wraps around three sides of his house until he could see, from behind the lacy veil of forest greenery, St. Joseph River burbling in a silvery wash of moonlight. He raised his eyes to the night sky. Six words thrummed in his mind.

I need to see the moon.

Indiana State Prison has two types of housing units. There is the dormitory unit, of which there are two at Indiana State Prison. Inside these buildings, between ninety and a hundred people live in two enormous open spaces, in the center of which is a lounge where dorm residents can read or watch television. Each prisoner is allotted a "pod" of personal space that measures six by six feet. Everything they own must be kept somewhere within this space. Whatever they do can be seen throughout the room by their fellow inmates and by correctional staff who stand guard. What these guys lose in privacy they gain in personal hygiene, for they are entitled to daily showers. But at night they can be vulnerable to foes. Some of them have been known to hit the bunks wearing makeshift protective gear created by piling stacks of magazines between their chests and their sleep shirts.

Another type of residential unit is the cell house, or cellblock, which ranks as one of the most sadistic perversions among housing concepts. Inside each house, cells stand back-to-back with only a narrow passageway between the rear walls. This passageway allows for plumbing and electrical maintenance of the cells.

Each cell is outfitted with a toilet and a sink. The prisoners who live in the cellblocks are permitted to shower every third day. The openings of the cells are made of steel bars that can be locked and unlocked individually or in unison by means of a giant roll bar. Thirty cells are lined up next to one another inside an immense, warehouse-like building.

What makes this form of housing particularly vulgar is that

the cells are stacked one on top of another four and five stories high. It looks as if the front walls of tiny units in a huge apartment complex have all been sliced off. Puppy mills, large-scale commercial breeding operations, are run on this concept. In puppy mills, dog kennels are stacked high and wide, and the animals inside know nothing but the wire door before them, the grids below their paws, and the incessant cacophony that rings in their ears.

Every cell house has its own identity. Men are sent to C Cell Block for lockdown, as punishment for irritating staff and for disruptive or violent behavior. Inside I Cell Block, which is the honor residence, prisoners are permitted to have cats. There is an Intensive Detention Unit, a prison-within-a-prison, in which men are isolated in single cells. They are not permitted to attend religious worship, all of their meals are delivered to the cells, and they are allowed one hour a day to exercise, after which they go right back into their cells. There is also a Protective Custody Unit for prisoners who are being harassed by other prisoners. And on X Row the cells are twice the size of a single cell, as if doubling the living space somehow compensates for the impending death sentence. All executions performed by the state of Indiana take place at Indiana State Prison.

One of Indiana State Prison's cell houses is the largest in Indiana and the second largest in the nation. Built in 1909, D Cell Block has 340 cells arranged on five tiers. Here Dave heard men attempting to play a game of chess from cells three floors apart. Two prisoners, each playing on a board inside his cell, would yell their moves to each other. Dave would hear one guy call out,

"Queen's knight to Kingside, rank four." The other guy would make that move on his board, and then, after deciding on his own move, call it out to his opponent.

Just outside the cells are balcony-like walkways, or ranges. To "walk the ranges" means to start at the flag deck, which is the first floor, and visit each prisoner by progressing in a methodical pattern from cell to cell and tier to tier on both of the mirror-image sides of each tier. Only people who have received special training in self-defense are permitted full access to the prison houses. Some chaplains and a select few volunteers use this privilege to visit with and counsel the men.

On the other side of the ranges is nothing but a corridor of space.

Not many people on the outside have a point of comparison to appreciate the sensory overload that is created inside an architectural nightmare such as one of these cell houses. The stench is unhealthy. An omnipresent din reverberates throughout the building. The noise pollution is mind-numbing.

In winter the heat rises and men on the lower decks shiver. In summer the heat rises and men on the upper decks swelter. Throughout his life, Father Dave has been impervious to changes in temperature. When others were mopping their brows, he was always comfortable in a three-piece suit. He was shocked to find that the oppressive heat on the upper tiers often caused him to become dizzy when he was walking the ranges.

Small windows checker the wall on the far side of the building. But the windows are barred, and the space between the ranges and that wall, about twelve feet, seems vast. So after the

5:30 lockdown, when prisoners peer out at the wall from between steel bars, they may catch a glimpse of indigo through the windows. Sometimes the mere hint of that inky firmament is enough to instigate a cascade of memories of what it was like to walk freely beneath the night sky.

But they surely never see the moon.

Education is simply the soul of a society as it passes from one genera-tion to another. —G. K. Chesterton

He who opens a school door, closes a prison. —Victor Hugo

4. Professor of Law

Father Dave's career in academe was a virtual immersion ex-perience in community, and the deaning years, a quarter-century apprenticeship in leadership. It was a middle period of growth and refinement that prepared him for his future prison ministry.

Father Dave says that becoming a priest was not a decision but a process. The process began during his professorship with the refinement of educational techniques he would call upon in teaching imprisoned men who would discover the joy of learning for the first time in their lives. The path toward the priesthood progressed in his deanship with the fine-tuning of discernment and peacemaking, skills he would utilize in bringing healing into the prison environment. The process continued to evolve with Dave's volunteer work for Habitat for Humanity and his work with homeless people, in the course of which he learned how to meet all kinds of people at the level of their needs. It advanced in Dave's presidency of the University of Notre Dame, Australia with international travel that revealed similarities as well as dif-ferences in how other cultures handle people who are deemed by their societies as the least, the last, the lost, and the lonely. Finally, as he was preparing to wrap up his career in academe, Dave would be introduced to prison work that would leave him standing on the threshold of his late-in-life career.

Dave and Barb returned to Notre Dame in 1970, which, for Dave, was like entering a vortex that engulfed him professionally and spiritually. From there he would spin forth prepared to comprehend and serve his brothers behind bars. The transformation began in the classroom.

D ave kicked off the first day of his career as a law school professor by announcing, "We will use the Socratic method in all of our classes. The one thing I'm going to specify is that in this classroom, I get to play Socrates."

He was joking, of course. The philosophy by which Dave was guided in his teaching was the principle of reciprocity. "I believe that the more you learn, the more you are capable of teaching," he explains when he is being serious. "And the more you teach, the more you learn. Early in my career I came up with the idea that we should videotape some of our lectures so that professors could review them for their own edification. When I watched my videotape, I realized that I would sometimes jump from this point to that point without bringing my students along with me. Coming to grips with what makes the subject flow was part of my own learning process.

"Hot Dog Inc. grew from that insight."

Hot Dog Inc. was a teaching device Dave created to help him take his students through the ins and outs of buying, selling, owning, and paying taxes on a corporate entity. Dave had always been impressed with Associate Dean Fernand N. "Tex" Dutile's philosophy on the art of teaching, which holds that "good teaching is not how much information a teacher conveys but rather how much the student remembers." Dave's teaching device became one of the ways that he made course material memorable.

More than forty years later, James E. "Jim" Dahl, who is an attorney-at-law at his own Chicago firm, Dahl & Bonadies LLC, says that those Hot Dog Inc. lessons are just as vivid to him now as they were when he was a student.

"Hot Dog Inc. was *wonderful* due to the continuity of an entity that would morph into all sorts of different corporate shapes depending on what Professor Link needed to teach us that day. One day Hot Dog Inc. would get burned down, and we'd explore whether the company was entitled to a casualty loss. Another day Hot Dog Inc. would have this kind of income and this kind of expenses, and we'd discuss which of them was or was not deductible."

Jim is a double-Domer who earned his BA in 1971 and his Juris Doctor in 1974. He was a first-year student the same year that Dave began teaching at Notre Dame.

"I was an econ major undergrad with a concentration in taxation, so I knew that I wanted to take tax in law school, and I took several courses from Dave. He was an exceptional teacher. He was comfortable in front of a classroom. He was engaging.

"There was a level of professionalism about Dave's classes. This was a lawyer teaching future lawyers, not a law professor teaching law students. He was never bashful about mentioning his background at Winston, Strawn, but he always approached it from a standpoint of 'This is not just theoretical; this is a real-world problem. I've had clients who had this problem.' Every day he conveyed to us that he wasn't just teaching us stuff so that we could learn it. He was teaching it to us so that we could help solve people's problems. We almost felt as if we were at that big firm with him. Without being stiff or formal, he conveyed seriousness and an expectation that our performance and our focus were the highest, and we felt as if we were being mentored by someone in a top-notch, first-class firm. He was cordial, friendly, and open, but he didn't need to be your buddy—he was the senior partner. He gave us a sense of what it means to be a lawyer."

Richard L. "Rich" Hill, who heads up the public finance group at Faegre Baker Daniels LLP, and serves as office leader of the firm's South Bend office, was also at Notre Dame Law School at the beginning of Dave's teaching career.

"Professor Link brought the energy of a practicing attorney to the way he taught. He'd show up in a very sharp tailored suit, very glamorous and well put together, and he moved all around the classroom as he taught. He brought a different style than someone who was just an academic. He was passionate, because he was teaching us about what he had practiced. And because he taught with such passion, he was teaching us so much more.

"I went into his classes expecting to get tax provisions or whatever. What I got instead was this profound sense of what is fair and what is not fair. He would ask, 'What is intended by this tax policy? Is this fair?' He understood it all so well, the time in class just flew by. He put the technical provisions into a larger context, as if he were hanging them on a tree. I did well because he taught it well."

Rich was sensitive to the political climate at Notre Dame Law School.

"Those were interesting times. There was a whole lot of turmoil in our country and on our campus. I came from Philadelphia [LaSalle University, BA, 1969], where my roommate and I had an apartment in which we would gather every evening with a bunch of other students to watch the six P.M. news for the casualty counts.

"During these times, the people entering the Law School were of two groups: those coming from an undergraduate experience and those coming from Vietnam. So you'd go out for a beer with your classmates, and some of them, like me, were conscientious objectors, and some of them had been shot at. The veterans may not have agreed with the conscientious objectors. But the Law School fostered a respectful environment. We were very aware that our faculty was neither liberal nor conservative. It was diverse. And that helped us to be accommodating of the myriad views that exist in the world. What happened there was a great amalgamation of faculty and students."

As a student, Rich gave volunteer assistance to legal aid services, and his passion for helping poor people who were underinformed about their legal rights continued after graduation.

"I started my practice in legal services as a juvenile court defender. I found myself sitting down at kitchen tables, usually with scared mothers and their sons, talking about the defense of children who would otherwise have been sent away to a boys' school. In 1974 I became the program director. There were five staff attorneys in one South Bend office. When I left in 1980 to work on the economic development of jobs for the city of South

Bend, the juvenile program had grown into a Northern Indiana program serving twenty-five counties with twenty-five lawyers.

"So many times there are potential points of intervention, opportunities where we can administer justice rather than win cases. Some lawyers love the thrill of the dispute. But I approach things from the Link point of view: *How can you bring everyone together and have them all be satisfied?*"

D ave accepted an associate deanship appointment in 1971, just one year after becoming a professor. In the meantime, Barbara and Nancy Shaffer picked up their friendship as if they had never parted. They started a book club, beginning with Fifty Books that Every Person Should Read Before Starting College, a list that one of Barbara's nuns had given her at St. Mary's High School. The book clubbers met once a month over lunch. Long before recycling became fashionable, Barbara started a tradition of recycling at these meetings.

Tom watched from his vantage in the associate dean's office as his friend took to a new career in academia, and he could not have been more pleased.

"Dave was a gifted teacher from the first day. One year into teaching law, he was a brilliant success. The students chose him Rookie of the Year."

Tom recounts a favorite vignette from 1971, the year the students were shunted to the old biology building while the Law School underwent remodeling.

"Dave taught in the old medical auditorium—a cavern of a room, steeply pitched so that students could lean forward and watch the teacher remove tumors. When the large tax class met there for the first time that fall, Dave greeted them in a long white coat. At his right hand was a full human skeleton hanging from a portable stand. Dave wheeled the skeleton to center stage. He said, 'This, ladies and gentlemen, is a taxpayer after audit.' Dave was truly in his element when he was teaching."

In 1974 Dave became acting dean. Even so, as Tom recalls, "Dave kept teaching just as many courses as he had when he was a professor. It was almost sad when he became dean."

Yes, but it was Tom who nudged Dave into the deanship.

By all accounts, Tom was a fine dean, yet his true calling lay elsewhere. Tom was a scholar.

Dave understood that Tom was frustrated. "Tom's most exceptional abilities were being wasted," Dave commented, "for he is one of those great thinkers who were born to analyze and write. He could analyze a legal question better than anyone else."

In 1975, after Tom made it clear he would like to shift the deanship to Dave, Father Ted called Dave to his office. He stoked Dave's fiery idealism with his vision of Notre Dame Law School becoming an international presence. Winston, Strawn, Smith and Patterson granted Dave an indefinite leave of absence that stands even now: "The longest leave of absence since the Prophet Elijah's chariot went upward in a cloud of smoke," Tom notes with a chuckle. Tom went back to teaching, research, and writing, and Dave assumed the helm.

What happened next was almost alchemical. Dave built upon a stellar faculty by luring some of the best and the brightest from around the world. Tom and Nancy summarized the magic of the

Law School during that era: "Dean Link was the optimist who always started with 'Yes.' But then a lot of other people would have to follow in his wake."

The spouses of the faculty were so supportive of the Notre Dame mission that they, too, became part of the charisma. Tex and Brigid Dutile became a powerful force in the life of the Law School as well as lifelong friends of the Links. The students, who were invited into the homes of the dean and associate deans for social events, couldn't help but be inspired by the camaraderie that was being modeled by the professors and their spouses.

A renaissance was under way at Notre Dame Law School.

America's present need is not heroics but healing; not nostrums but normalcy; not revolution but restoration.

—President Warren G. Harding

5. THE DEAN WHO DREAMED OF HEALING

As dean of the Law School, Dave attended receptions, meet and greets, and formal affairs all over the world. At one cocktail party he was talking to a couple of people when the hostess approached, apologized for interrupting, and explained that one of her guests wanted to meet Dean Link. Pulling Dave from the group, she led him across the room and introduced him to attorney-at-law and philanthropist William H. "Bill" Gates Sr.

Mr. Gates smiled broadly, stuck out his hand, and told Dave that he was intrigued by the philosophy by which Dean Link was guiding the Notre Dame Law School. Mr. Gates peppered Dave with questions. Was it true that Dave viewed law as a healing profession? Where had he gotten this notion? How was he able to incorporate this philosophy into the daily workings of the Law School? What kind of reception had this idea received from faculty and students? Mr. Gates invited Dave to visit the Gates Compound in Medina, Washington, to explore these ideas in greater depth.

Father Ted Hesburgh's dream of developing an internationally respected Law School became a reality in large part due to Dean Link's view of the law as a healing profession. The

philosophy was attractive to faculty and students alike, and it set
Notre Dame apart from other law schools. It became the framework by which Notre Dame educated cutting-edge, effective,
ethical attorneys.

Mohandas K. Gandhi had helped to pave the way in the ar-
ticulation of this point of view when in 1893–94, in Pretoria,
South Africa, he represented his client Dada Abdulla in a complex business dispute. In his *Autobiography*, *The Story of My Experiments with Truth*, Gandhi explained the profound impact this case
had on his understanding of the true purpose of the practice of
law. He wrote, "I had learnt to find out the better side of human
nature and to enter men's hearts. I realized that the true function
of a lawyer was to unite parties riven asunder. The lesson was so
indelibly burnt into me that a large part of my time during the
twenty years of my practice as a lawyer was occupied in bringing
about private compromises of hundreds of cases. I lost nothing
thereby—not even money, certainly not my soul."

In the late 1960s one early case in Dave's Chicago practice
convinced Dave that dispute resolution, in which parties find
mutually agreeable terms to retire litigious issues out of court,
was the best way to practice. He had been asked to oversee the
liquidation of a successful corporation owned by two brothers.
One way of collecting his legal fees would have been to take care
of the paperwork and get the liquidation done as equitably as possible. But Dave was more proactive. He visited the town where
the company was located and toured the facilities. He met with
both brothers and unearthed their twin passions for the company.
Dave pressed them to think about what they would do every day
when the company belonged to someone else. Were they looking

forward to retirement? Did they have a desire to travel or take up a hobby? They answered no to all of these questions. Confronting the starkness of not belonging to something bigger than themselves caused the brothers to pause. Maybe liquidation was not in their best interests after all.

In the end, Dave was able to broker a plan in which the company was divided into different divisions that were managed by each brother according to his area of expertise and interests. It was an astute solution for the client (which was the company), the brothers, and their families.

In 1983 Dave was already aboard the healing train when he attended an American Bar Association midyear meeting in New Orleans, Louisiana. Under discussion was the need to solve the problem of the negative image of attorneys that prevailed in the public sector. Should the ABA initiate a campaign to deal with the crisis in the profession by hiring a public relations firm?

Chief Justice Warren E. Burger challenged the group to think about the problem in a different way. Historically, he said, the original role of lawyers was to heal social conflict. He suggested that when lawyers got back to fulfilling that role in society the public's view of them as professionals would self-correct.

It was a definitive moment in Dave's life. From that day forward, he would give conscious consideration to the healing potential in personal and professional decisions he made as well as in the actions he performed.

After serving for one year as acting dean, Dave accepted the deanship in 1975. He had inherited a bare-bones crew. He was in dire need of help in getting his administration off the ground. He was looking for someone with solid administrative experience. The provost suggested that Captain William O. "Bill" McLean would be perfect for the position.

Captain McLean had served as a United States Navy pilot for thirty-two years before being recruited to direct the Reserve Officer Training Corp (ROTC) at the University of Notre Dame. He came to the university in 1972 with an outstanding reputation for, among other things, his work in promoting peace, having served the country as one of the principal military negotiators at the Strategic Arms Limitation Talks (SALT I). Bill was neither a lawyer nor a Catholic, yet three years later, in a career change no bookie would have taken as a bet, the captain traded gold-embroidered oak leaves and acorns to wear the cap of assistant and, not long afterward, associate dean of Notre Dame Law School.

It was Dave's initial opinion that the person who filled this position would have to be a lawyer. The fact that Captain McLean was not an attorney suggested to the new dean that the captain might be helpful to the Law School on a temporary basis. With these parameters in mind, Dave asked the captain to meet with him at the Law School.

Captain McLean came to the interview aware that the new dean was seeking to put together a top-drawer cabinet. "After talking with Dave for fifteen minutes or so," Bill recollects, "I knew that I belonged with this guy."

The feeling was mutual. Bill's "temporary" appointment lasted eighteen years.

Bill looks back on his Law School career and says, "I never once felt like a petunia in an onion patch. I was Dave's assistant,

but I never felt like a second fiddle. Both of us were naval officers. That was part of the good fit. We know how the navy functions and we live by those standards, and so talking with Dave
came easy. We met at least three to five times a week, if not a
couple times a day. From the beginning we had very good communication. We clicked in that regard. His was not a deanship of
memos; his door was always open. In fact, everybody's door was
always open—and *that* is a feature of our success that others can
duplicate.

"We made the cover of a national magazine. We were ranked
seventeenth out of more than 140 law schools in the nation. The
Law School grew in stature both within the university and beyond under Dave's collegial leadership, which I had the privilege
of participating in and watching from an inside perspective."

The concept of the healing function of law was embraced in
every class on a daily basis. In addition, Dave and the Admissions Committee made decisions on whom to admit and how
to mentor the students from this perspective. Dave sometimes
invoked his right to overrule the Admissions Committee when
he believed that a student whom they were inclined to turn away
truly belonged in the community. One student whom Dean Link
championed was Patrick Brennan.

Patrick had fallen in love with Notre Dame during the fall
of 1988, when his father, William Brennan, a fan since his Baltimore boyhood, invited his youngest child to join him in following what promised to be an exciting Fighting Irish football
season. Together, father and son watched every game but the one
that was not televised on the East Coast. At some point during

that 12–0 national championship season, Patrick was inspired with the notion of attending law school at Notre Dame, and he vowed that he would do whatever it took to get there.

Until that time Patrick had been a classic underachiever. But he launched a ferocious attack on his college studies, and he got that ship turned around. He finished strong at the University of Maryland, filled out his Notre Dame Law School application, and decided that nothing less than delivering it by hand would suffice.

On Sunday, January 30, 1994, at twenty-five years of age, Patrick boarded an airplane for the first time in his life. He flew into Chicago Midway International Airport, rented a car, and drove in blizzard conditions to South Bend. The road was all his when he turned from Angela Boulevard onto Notre Dame Avenue. There it was, straight ahead: the golden dome and, atop, *Notre Dame du Lac.* He pulled to a stop just across from Cedar Grove Cemetery, reached for the early generation mobile phone with which the rental vehicle had been equipped, and dialed home. Tears were streaming down his face as he told his parents, "I might not get in this year. I might not get in next year. It might take three years before I get here. It might take a lifetime before I get here. But this is home! And I'm going to find some way to get here."

A couple of months later Patrick was crushed when he received a letter that thanked him for applying and then went on to state that the class roster had been filled. His reaction was to make an appointment to meet with the dean. "My expectation was that my interview with the dean would center on the mechanics of the application process. Yet within moments of being introduced I sensed that Dean Link cared about me not merely as an applicant but as a person."

For ninety minutes Patrick and the dean discussed fundamental things in life. They talked about their families and about what had brought each of them to this place. Dean Link also advised Patrick to work on raising his LSAT scores. To that end, he told Patrick about a complex intelligence game called the WFF 'N PROOF, a game that would enable Patrick to practice and improve his logic skills. At the end of the meeting, Dean Link handed him his business card and said, "I'd like to see you apply again next year." Patrick held on to that card as if it were a talisman.

Patrick practiced like mad and was gratified by higher LSAT scores. Yet his reapplication earned him a place on the waiting list. Having a keen appreciation that an applicant who had been once rejected and subsequently wait-listed had no business bothering a busy academic, Patrick nevertheless made another appointment to meet with the dean. "At our meeting some days later, Dean Link's knowledge of my situation showed me that he was invested in my case and that, in fact, he cared a great deal about the course of my life."

Admitting that following this plan held a certain amount of risk, Dean Link advised Patrick that he should stay in constant touch with the admissions office. Again, Patrick followed the dean's advice. Every week from mid-April through late August, Patrick placed a call to Director of Admissions Anne Hamilton. He would ask, "Where am I on the wait list?" or "What's my status this week?" and then they would talk for a moment or two.

On the morning of August 25, 1995, Patrick woke with a

heart aflame with longing. It was the last Friday in August. Orientation weekend. He dreaded placing his call to Ms. Hamilton. She was gentle. He could hear in her voice that this was hard for her, too. "Your status on the wait list is unchanged," he heard her say, and the rest was a blur.

The next morning, talking with his parents over breakfast, Patrick tried to make sense of everything. He had believed that his personal destiny was supposed to be played out at Notre Dame. Obviously, he had been wrong. When he broke down sobbing, his father stated with inexplicable conviction, "They're going to call."

Patrick trudged through the day. In an attempt to distract him, his parents made a plan to take him out to dinner. At six-thirty William had just walked out into the driveway and Patrick was leaving the house with his mother, Beverly, when the phone rang. Beverly turned to look at her son, and the fullness of the expression on her face was devastating.

Patrick picked up the receiver. It was Anne Hamilton.

"I'm calling on behalf of Dean Link. Dean Link would like to know if you still want to be a member of the class."

He crumbled. Dimly aware that he must accept the offer before it could be rescinded, he was somehow able to choke out an inelegant but effective acceptance.

"Yes."

William and Beverly helped their son gather his things and pack his car. By Sunday night Patrick was moving into a dorm room at Notre Dame. And things went well for Patrick. He worked hard. He got good grades. He loved what he was learning. But in April 1997, just as he was in the midst of preparing for his second-year second-semester finals, everything fell apart.

Patrick was pushing hard. He would study until he could take it no more, then stave off complete collapse by sleeping for a few hours. On the Saturday two weeks before finals, he fell asleep at 8:00 in the evening for what was supposed to be a two-hour nap. He was awakened at 2:30 in the morning by a sharp, searing pain in his head. When he opened his eyes, the room was spinning so badly he couldn't tell the ceiling from the floor. He tried to stand. He collapsed in a heap on the floor and was ill with projectile vomiting that lasted fifteen minutes before the horrific event subsided.

He struggled to hold it together. But life became a torturous hell due to repeated episodes of violent illness. Finally, at the insistence of Dean Link, Patrick suspended his studies and was put on a flight to Baltimore. Upon his arrival, an emergency MRI revealed a brain tumor. He was rushed into surgical intensive care at the Greater Baltimore Medical Center. Surgery was scheduled for first thing in the morning. He was handed a pen so that he could sign grim legal disclosures warning that he very well might die during surgery.

"What are my other treatment options?" he asked.

"There are none," he was told.

He signed.

Patrick's family gathered. They brought to the hospital a couple of his most prized possessions. Chief among them was the letter of admission that had been signed by David T. Link, Joseph A. Matson Dean of the University of Notre Dame Law School.

His parents and siblings kept an all-night vigil, surrounding Patrick with love, prayer, and tears.

Patrick's were the only dry eyes in the group. He attributes his calm acceptance to the examples he had been shown by Dean Link and the other inspirational leaders he had met at Notre Dame Law School.

"I had been convinced of no less than the certainty of God's presence in my life," says Patrick. "It was easy to keep my composure. If I'd never been a student in the Notre Dame Law School, if I'd never come to this campus, if I'd never met David Link, then I would have flipped out like everyone else. For me, life and death had become analogous to life before Notre Dame Law School as compared with life after Notre Dame Law School.

"We all have a general sense of what heaven is going to be like—the people we hope to meet and just how great it's going to be. And yet we know that we do not have the capacity to appreciate what it will be like. Heaven is so immense and so good, our brains cannot imagine just how good it will be.

"Notre Dame Law School was like that for me. It was so big, and it was so wonderful, and I loved it so much, and I admired and appreciated Dean Link and that entire building full of heroes so much, I did not possess the capacity to appreciate its goodness until I got there."

Patrick survived eight and a half hours of emergency brain surgery during which a plum-sized medulloblastoma was removed. He spent the next several months enduring daily outpatient brain and spinal radiation therapy at the Johns Hopkins Hospital. Through it all, his sole ambition was to reclaim his hard-earned place inside the classrooms at Notre Dame Law School. When he returned to campus, Patrick confided a myriad of misgivings to his dean. He was not sure that his physical condition would allow him to get up and over a mountain of work that to him looked unscalable. Dean Link told him, "Just get back in the game."

Patrick earned his Juris Doctor in 1998. After commencement, he returned to Baltimore with reluctance, unable to imagine life without Notre Dame in it. He scoured the Internet for career openings at Notre Dame, applied for a position as director of gift planning there, and was ecstatic when he landed the job.

Patrick has made a permanent home for himself in South Bend. He still gets a thrill every time he drives up Notre Dame Avenue and sees Our Lady standing on top of the golden dome. It is rare that Patrick shares his remarkable story. But as he travels across the country and meets with potential donors, he sometimes intuits that what he understands to be the essence of the university must be conveyed with the telling of his personal narrative. Then he will fight his way through what is always an emotional recounting of the dean who dreamed of healing.

Every year Patrick flies to Baltimore for a checkup at Johns Hopkins. Short though these visits to his parents and siblings may be, there are more smiles than tears in their good-byes. Everyone understands that, as far as Patrick is concerned, all roads and airways lead to Notre Dame. There is nowhere else he would rather be, and there is nothing else he would rather do than continue being of service to his beloved Notre Dame.

Having launched his professional career in South Bend, Rich Hill was well situated to observe developments in the Law

School under Dave's deanship. Rich characterizes his former professor as "the quiet servant leader" and says of what he calls the Link era, "What I saw was the exercise of meaningful leadership."

Binding the Notre Dame Law School faculty, which was anything but homogenous, required adept leadership. Two professors in particular, Charles Edward "Charlie" Rice and Joseph P. "Joe" Bauer, represented opposite ends of the political spectrum. Charlie Rice came on board in 1969, not long after having founded the Conservative Party of New York State and serving as general counsel of the John Birch Society. Joe Bauer, who was famous as a card-carrying member of the American Civil Liberties Union, joined the faculty in 1973. The rest of the faculty fell along the continuum between the polarities represented by these two men. That the faculty held their dean in high regard is evidenced by the way his performance was rated. Every five years law school faculties are charged with the responsibility of submitting yea or nay votes on their deans. Despite the vast differences in the politics and philosophies of the faculty members, each of the four times the Notre Dame Law School faculty considered Dave Link, the vote to retain Dave as dean was unanimous.

Rich offers his take on why.

"There are many people who, as you get closer, you find out that there is a myth. They are less of a reality, more just a representation. With Dave it's directly opposite. With Dave there is an inverse proportion to what typically happens. With Dave there is even more there than you thought."

Jim Dahl agrees. "This business of 'the Notre Dame lawyer' . . . someone for whom integrity comes first, then intellect, then imagination . . . This notion that the law is a noble profession, here to resolve not create conflict . . . That all came out of Dave Link's pulpit.

"It all starts with the clarity of his vision, this idea of 'the Notre Dame Lawyer.' In fact, this is what gets articulated with Dave Link's deanship: that Notre Dame lawyers are different. That we're more socially aware. That it's not just about success and winning; it's about how we succeed and how we win, and then where we apply those gifts. Notre Dame lawyers are the ones who practice law in a more ethical and more sensitive way. These are not going to be the guys who gouge clients or condone a 'whatever it takes' mentality."

During the deaning years, Dave and Barb were blessed with two more additions to the family. First, many prayers were answered when Barbara became pregnant in 1973. Given what had happened with Little Barbara, there was concern that this baby might need a full blood transfusion, and the pregnancy was considered high risk. Dave and Barb traveled more than a hundred miles from South Bend to Evanston, Illinois, for Barb's prenatal checkups. An extensive team of obstetrical and neonatal specialists assembled when Barbara was admitted to the hospital for labor and delivery. Dave paced and prayed in the father's waiting room.

After some time Dave saw two men in surgical scrubs push through the swinging double doors; he stopped dead in his tracks and held his breath. Whipping off his surgical mask, one of the doctors was overheard to say to the other, "Well, we can unhook all those damn machines in there. That's the healthiest kid I've ever seen," and Dave's heart soared.

"From the moment that we lost Little Barbara," says Father Dave, "Barb and I asked God to bless us with another child. Teran Elizabeth, born five years after we buried Little Barbara, was never an afterthought. She was a constant thought."

The final addition to this generation of Links came from South America in 1990. By this time Teran was in high school and all the other children were out of the house and living on their own. Dave and Barb volunteered to host a foreign exchange student who was the same age as Teran, and they were blessed with a chosen daughter as a result.

Patricia "Pato" Perez came to South Bend from Bogotá, Colombia. By the time she returned to South America, the Links considered Pato one of them, for she completed the family in a way that just felt right. In future years, Pato would travel from Colombia to reconvene with the Links as often as possible. After she was married, her husband was also considered part of the family; when she became a mother, her two children were added into the grandchild roll call.

Over the course of thirty years as an academic, Dave traveled to and worked in Australia, South Africa, Japan, Russia, England, Chile, Mexico, Canada, Israel/Palestine, Jordan, and Italy. He wore the hats of university professor, dean, provost, and president.

But those were Dave Link's day jobs. What he did after hours is another story.

Captain McLean, who worked beside Dave most of the years

of Dave's deanship, admires without reservation the man he nicknamed "Skipper." He also admires the way that the Skipper of USS *NDLS* conducted his life.

"Dave would sit in the office and work all day and work hard. When five o'clock came and the rest of us went home, he went to do things for the community and for the city government. From the time I first knew him, Dave always lived a double life of service."

Since the early years of the marriage, Barbara and the children had waited until Dave arrived home from work before they shared dinner together as a family. So when Dave left the law school, he usually headed home for dinner and a little bit of time with Barbara and his family. But before the setting of the sun, more often than not, he took off his double-breasted suits and Brooks Brothers ties, changed into blue jeans and a shirt, rolled up his sleeves, and went to work all over again.

"Then the King will say to those on His right hand, 'Come, you blessed of My Father, inherit the kingdom prepared for you from the foundation of the world: for I was hungry and you gave Me food; I was thirsty and you gave Me drink; I was a stranger and you took Me in; I was naked and you clothed Me; I was sick and you visited Me; I was in prison and you came to Me.' Then the righteous will answer Him, saying, 'Lord, when did we see You hungry and feed You, or thirsty and give You drink? When did we see You a stranger and take You in, or naked and clothe You? Or when did we see You sick, or in prison, and come to You?' And the King will answer and say to them, 'Assuredly, I say to you, inasmuch as you did it to one of the least of these My brethren, you did it to Me.' "   —Matthew 25:34–40

---

6. Subterranean No More

One of Dave's after-hours passions was volunteering for Habitat for Humanity, an ecumenical nonprofit that has helped to build more than 500,000 homes for people all over the world. Founded in 1976 by Millard and Linda Fuller, Habitat achieved international renown with the promotion it received from its adoptive parents, President Jimmy and Rosalynn Carter.

Dave was brought into the Habitat family by architect and humanitarian LeRoy S. Troyer, whose firm, the Troyer Group, has created two of South Bend's prides: the College Football Hall of Fame; and Southfield Village, which is a national model for a housing trend known as intergenerational living. LeRoy built his architectural firm around two core concepts. First, Troyer structures are designed to rest harmoniously in their environment. Second, they are built with the motive of ending poverty housing, that is, the substandard public housing in which people below the poverty level are forced to live.

LeRoy found a niche within the Habitat family and has championed them ever since. He met Dean Link at a Notre Dame function, extended an invitation to Dave, and the dean was on-site at the very next building project. Dave pitched in on a number of local and regional projects. As the houses were being constructed, Dave and LeRoy were building a lasting friendship.

Dave also joined the group that traveled across the nation and internationally to build Jimmy Carter Works Projects. From 1995 to 2002 Dave joined five of these project crews, including one in Vác, Hungary. One night in Vác, Dave and some of the house captains gathered together with President Carter in the former president's anteroom and talked of many things, including monuments around the world. Carter observed that, to his knowledge, no monument had ever been built to honor Jesus, who was, he said, "the greatest man who has ever lived." That moment marked the conception of a living monument they would create and christen Nazareth Village. A portion of the city of Nazareth in Israel would be rebuilt to look just as it had when Jesus was born. Volunteers in period dress would come and perform the same daily chores and activities that had occupied villagers during Jesus's lifetime. Dave served as the initial chair of the board. A framed picture of Nazareth Village occupies a place of honor over the piano in Dave's South Bend residence.

———

A lthough Dave loved participating in Habitat projects, his work with the homeless of South Bend served as an apprenticeship for his prison ministry. This work showed him that simple human connection often resuscitates hope in those who have given up.

Helping the poor was woven into the daily fabric of the Link household, and so trying to pinpoint a definitive moment that marked the beginning of Dave's efforts on behalf of the homeless is like trying to localize the edge of fog. Yet one night stands out.

It was a Saturday in the month of January 1986. Dave had just stepped out into a heavy snowfall when he turned to catch one more look at Barbara. She was leaning over the kitchen sink so that he could see her waving through the frosty window. Dave smiled and waved back, then trudged through the shoveled path to the garage. Mindful of the trees encroaching on either side, he drove with caution down the long, curving driveway.

He drove to Michigan Avenue in downtown South Bend, where he would be supervising a group of student volunteers who were caring for homeless men. Dave knew from experience that he would be busy. When frigid northwest winds whip over Lake Michigan, bringing lake-effect blizzards to the city, the homeless people he had come to know on a first-name basis were sure to file into the lower level of the Maranatha Temple. Here they would find a cot on which to sleep and shelter from the storm. In the morning Dave and the students would serve coffee and doughnuts to fortify their guests before the men embarked on another long day of shivering in the streets of South Bend.

On this particular Saturday night, six students from the University of Notre Dame and St. Mary's College braved the weather to join Dave. Together Dean Link and the students worked until all the men were bedded down for the night. Outside a relentless snowfall muffled the sounds of the city. Inside the subterranean haven, a hibernal hush descended.

It was nearly eleven P.M. when the arrival of a latecomer disturbed the tranquility. The man was old. He was dirty. He was drunk. And he was someone Dave had never seen before.

Dave helped the stranger to an empty cot. The man plopped down, grunting as he hit bottom, and the odious stench of stale alcohol puffed from his mouth. He leaned over to unlace his boots, but the effort was too much for him. He tipped over and would have conked his head except that Dave was quick enough to come between him and the floor. No sooner had Dave propped the old fellow into an upright position than the stranger bent to untie his bootlaces. Again Dave caught the man before he cracked his skull on the floor. Deciding that either he was going to do the job himself or this guy was going to get a concussion, Dave helped the stranger lie back on the cot.

Dave blanketed the old man from his neck to his knees, then set about working the laces free. Dave tugged until the man's boots came off. He was dismayed to find soaking wet socks and, beneath them, feet that were showing signs of frostbite. He turned to a student.

"I need a pan of cold water and a stack of towels," he directed. "Each time I ask you to refill the pan, I want you to fill it with water that is a little bit warmer than it was in the previous pan. We have to try to save this man's toes."

Unaware of time, Dave washed the feet of the slumbering drunkard over and over again. When he was satisfied that full circulation had been restored, he asked another student volunteer to bring him a pair of dry socks. Dave worked the socks over the man's now-pink feet, then pulled the blanket all the way down to cover them. He stood and began to walk away.

The old man roused himself enough to grab Dave by the leg, calling out as he did so, "Can I ask you a question?"

Dave turned, surprised that the stranger was awake.

"Sure," he answered. "What do you want to know?"

"Does God still love me?"

A ripple of recognition raced through Dave's entire being.

"Yes," he answered, slowly, thoughtfully. "God still loves you."

"Does God still love me even when I drink too much, like tonight?"

"God's love is unconditional. God loves all of us. He loves everyone in this room no matter what has happened in their lives."

The next morning, the stranger vanished, never again to be seen by Dave or any of the volunteers.

Later, one of the students asked, "Dean Link, did you know that old man? It certainly seemed that he knew you."

Dave's gaze shifted away from the student's face, and for a few long seconds he stared somewhere off into the middle distance.

Finally, he said, "I have never seen that man before. But I think I know who he is. And I think that he knows all of us."

From that night on, Dave had an abiding affinity for the parable of the washing of the feet. And he made up his mind to do something about homelessness in South Bend.

———

H e couldn't have done it without the help of a friend.

It was D'Arcy Chisholm who had shown him the ropes in the basement of the Maranatha Temple. D'Arcy, whose background was in real estate, was serving as associate director for the Center for Pastoral Care at the University of Notre Dame when he and Dave met. Although their personalities could not have been more different, they became great friends and were known affectionately within the Notre Dame community as "the Odd Couple." D'Arcy's bold business acumen, which was the perfect Oscar Madison foil for Dave's Felix Unger–like reticence, would feature prominently in the realization of Dave's dream of creating a better place for the homeless to be homeless in South Bend.

Across the street from the Maranatha Temple was an abandoned building. In better times 813 South Michigan Street, a three-story, ninety-thousand-square-foot structure, had been the home of Gilbert's Mens' Clothing Store. After Gilbert's closed its South Bend retail outlet, the property had been sold to a shoe company with out-of-state headquarters. Having been abandoned for more than eight years, the building and its environs had deteriorated into a deplorable state.

It was Dave's idea to purchase the building and turn it into a state-of-the-art homeless center. He envisioned a place where South Bend's homeless citizens could be housed and fed, a place where they could get help in breaking the cycles of dependency, violence, addiction, and homelessness. He wanted to create a clean, safe, campus-like environment in which people could discover and develop their personal giftedness.

But there was a problem. When Dave cast his eye across

the street from the Maranatha Temple to the abandoned Gilbert's building and decided that it had great potential to become the center of his dreams, the asking price of the property was $450,000.

D'Arcy loved Dave's idea and relished a good real estate tussle, so he began working a deal. Along with a pledge of $15,000—each of them put up $7,500 of personal funds—D'Arcy composed a letter in which he explained the charitable nature of their endeavor and offered the owners $60,000 to buy the building.

Dave was horrified. "You can't offer them $60,000 for that building," he protested. "That's embarrassing!"

D'Arcy just smiled and sent the letter.

The response they received was mercifully polite. *You must have misread . . . The property is listed at $450,000 . . . but since this will be a charity . . . we are hereby cutting our price to $350,000.*

D'Arcy made an $80,000 counteroffer and plotted the next move. He and Dave would take pictures of the dilapidated property. The photographs would be included along with their next letter and final offer. D'Arcy insisted that the two of them take a camera into the midst of an area one would never call a neighborhood, because there were no neighbors here. No. This place was an urban wasteland. This was where bums clutching bottles covered in brown bags came to curl up in a corner, and if they were lucky as they shuffled to their favorite abandoned doorways, along the way they would find a piece of cardboard, as good a mattress as they could hope for.

Shaking his head, Dave said, "I can't believe that I am out here with you and we are doing what we are doing."

D'Arcy just laughed.

D'Arcy included the photos with his next letter. *Obviously, being absentee landlords,* he wrote, *you are not aware of just how much this place has disintegrated. Bums sleep in the doorways; adjacent parking and empty lots are littered with trash, discarded needles, broken bottles, etc., etc. As you can see from the enclosed photographs, this property is deteriorating day by day.* D'Arcy made his final offer: *The building has been on the market for eight years. You can keep the earnest money that Dave and I have already paid. We have borrowed $100,000 from the federal government. Closing costs will be $4,000.00. What this means is that we are offering you $96,000 for the property, take it or leave it.*

They took it.

In working on some of the problems of homelessness in South Bend, it was as if Dave was undertaking postgraduate-level studies on poverty. He learned that one consequence of spending successive generations in poverty was the inheritance of life skills so counterproductive that they weren't skills at all. For example, instead of rationality as a strategy for dealing with disappointment, these people inherited rage. Abuse was what they had seen and suffered, so they learned not the art of nurturing but how to abuse. Left to their own devices in maneuvering survival at the edges of the American dream, many homeless people are sick or disabled or both. Their untreated physical illnesses and mental disorders shatter any hope of hearth and home. Having been failed by their parents, teachers, communities, and government, oftentimes these people finished off the job by failing themselves, turning to substance abuse as a result of an organic-based disease, or as an escape, or in a futile effort to lash out at the world in general.

Dave and Barbara looked into the faces of these people and saw not the least. Not the last. Not the lost. They saw the lonely.

They raised their children in a culture of compassion. Back when the Links lived in Wilmette, young David, Mary, and Maureen considered little Carl Witherspoon just another kid in the house. Sometimes he was that annoying brother who was on your bike when you wanted to ride it. He was never considered more special than they were, but neither was he treated any less special. In the Link household Carl was an equal.

Talk around the Link dinner table often gravitated to the needs of less privileged communities. Dave and Barb's children grew up involved in youth groups and in performing community service of all kinds.

Even so, there was much that the kids did not know. For example, growing up, Teran knew that her father spent Saturday nights at the Maranatha Temple. But she was unaware that he was at the Temple on many weeknights as well.

Teran's lack of awareness was due at least in part to her parents' unanimity on the issue of service to the less fortunate. In this particular case, it meant that her father was the designated half of Team Dave and Barb that would be present overnight with the homeless men, while her mother played her part from home. Their partnership became a system in which volunteerism was performed so quietly, like the current running below the surface of a frozen river, it could almost go unnoticed.

Teran often found herself sharing a seat in the family car with elderly shut-ins whom her mother took back and forth to medical appointments, the grocery store, or the pharmacy. She was also the littlest volunteer every time her mother slipped away to 532 South Michigan Street, where Barbara was a familiar presence at Hope Rescue Mission. Teran remembers feeling uneasy sitting in the midst of strangers who looked, to her, somehow different, while her mother was busy helping in the preparation and serving of meals. But Teran also remembers feeling secure enough to trust that those moments of disquiet would be resolved. She knew for certain that eventually her mother would bring her own plate to the table, sit down, and break bread with those whom she had just served. With her mother by her side, those faint pangs of fear dissolved. Teran was freed to anticipate with elation the ritual that was her favorite part of the evening. After everyone had eaten, together they joined in the singing of "Amazing Grace."

One of the more devastating aspects of concentrated poverty is spatial mismatch, a term social scientists use to describe the conundrum faced by people who need jobs but who cannot access job opportunities owing to the physical distance between workers and the workplace. Inner-city dwellers are isolated from the grapevine that connects job openings with willing workers. Lack of transportation prevents the unemployed from being able to seek interviews for those jobs. Jobs remain out of reach for these already disadvantaged people who, just like the buildings in which businesses once thrived, were abandoned when urban redevelopment and shopping malls shifted locales away from the cities. Thus a geographical disconnect is created between these potential workers and the work that they can perform.

Isolation affects all aspects of life, not just employment.

For the poor, education that is commensurate with the national standards, community recreation programs, quality childcare, and health care services are no more real than the giants of Don Quixote's windmill delusions. So, when Dave and D'Arcy set about putting the "ing's" into their dream—plumbing, heating, cooling, bedding, cooking, feeding, clothing, training, and financing the renovations—Dave had a vision of a transformative experience for the homeless that would resolve the core problem of isolation that this population faces.

There are three parts to the mission statement of the Center for the Homeless, South Bend. First, the center focuses on helping people break the cycle of homelessness. Second, the center attempts to heal disparity with familiarity by matching up those who have jobs, skills, and time with those who are in need of mentoring, and each becomes familiar with the other on a person-to-person basis. Third, the center stands as a premier model of service to the homeless by operating on the principle that the larger community needs and benefits from the homeless community as much as the homeless community needs and benefits from the larger community.

Luckily, the center has been blessed with a strong working partnership with the University of Notre Dame. From financial backing to job opportunities for guests of the center, renovations, staffing, and a steady source of assistance from student volunteers, Notre Dame has been integral in making the dream a reality. But the community at large also rallied around the project in a dramatic way after a disaster concentrated the attention of South Bend's citizens on the renovations that were being done at the old Gilbert's building.

On December 16, 1988, an early-morning fire raged through the Morningside Hotel, a 105-room, four-story residential hotel located in downtown South Bend. One man lost his life. Several men and women were seriously injured. Over a hundred people were rendered helpless and homeless.

That same day Barbara was making final preparations for a faculty Christmas party at the Link home when the evening news came on. On the family's small kitchen television the local broadcast featured a story on what had been a horrendous two-alarm fire. Reporters described barefooted residents having to flee the fire wearing nightclothes. Coverage included an interview with her denim-clad David, who was knee-deep in cleaning, painting, and assembling beds at the Center for the Homeless, which hadn't yet opened. Dave, responding to an urgent plea from South Bend mayor (subsequently governor of Indiana) Joseph Kernan, made a passionate appeal to the community, asking that everyone "please call this phone number" if they have donations of any kind—food, clothing, anything.

From another room in the house, Teran heard her mother exclaim, "WHAT?"

The number that David recited and that was plastered across the television screen was the telephone number for the Link residence.

Dave knew that the center was far from being ready to open its doors to the public. But the need was now, and the need was great. His earnest appeal to the citizens of South Bend was made through the newspapers, over the radio, and on local television stations. That evening he answered the question in Barbara's eyes with his best Johnny Carson grin and a rhetorical question of his own: "What other number was there to give?"

Teran answered the home phone for two days straight.

The community's response to the crisis was nimble and generous. At the center, members of the youth group to which Teran belonged were stunned at the piles of food, clothing, and gifts that appeared as if they had been delivered by magic to 813 South Michigan Street. While the teens sorted through the donations, Teran's father and other volunteers worked around the clock. The Center for the Homeless, South Bend was able to open its doors to just under a hundred guests fewer than twelve hours after the fire, proof that the "better angels of our nature" that President Abraham Lincoln referenced in his first inaugural address were the first responders to Dave's call for help.

An Associated Press story that ran in newspapers across the country reported the tremendous outpouring of community support for the homeless center. The final sentence of the article quoted "center volunteer David T. Link," who told of someone walking in off the street with a $1,000 check made out to the center.

"Center volunteer" was true in one sense. The interviewee never informed the reporter that he was the cofounder of the new center and that he was dean of the University of Notre Dame Law School.

Two years after the fire forced the premature opening of the center, twenty-nine-year-old Louis M. "Lou" Nanni, ND '84, MA '88, was recruited as the new executive director. The center had been floundering owing to a succession of ineffective directors; when Lou arrived, he walked into some epic challenges. In the eight years that he devoted to the center, Lou cultivated a robust volunteer-empowered model. He also excelled at "community matchmaking." He put together partnerships that were designed to break down the barriers that divide people socioeconomically, racially, ethnically, and educationally. What was significant and new about the center's approach to homelessness was how Lou was able to accomplish this. He set about fostering meaningful interpersonal relationships between people who stood on opposite sides of the divide.

Lou, who now serves the University of Notre Dame as vice president for university relations, says that he believed then, as now, that "everybody is looking for two things in life: joy and meaning. And so when we were able to get people involved on a personal level, they weren't thinking about abstract concepts any longer. They were thinking about actual human beings, people whose names they knew, people they grew to care about. This model allows for each person to discover the other's God-given dignity and potential. Not only was our common humanity furthered, but everybody was enriched in the process."

Under Lou's direction, the center achieved a national reputation for its pioneering model and was held in such regard that Lou was asked to testify before a joint session of Congress as part of a congressional debate on welfare reform.

Visitors from all over the country came in a steady stream to tour the center. Cities across North America— Miami, Honolulu, Salt Lake City, and Ottowa, Canada—invited Lou to come and teach them how they could establish similar centers. Every time he accepted such an invitation, Lou brought with him one or two center guests so that they could tell their personal stories at the seminars.

Lou says, "The political left thinks that you can throw money at problems raised by the outcasts, the people who are living in the margins. The political right thinks that you can legislate solutions. The fact of the matter is, this is labor-intensive work and it is personal. And so the question is not *where* do we start in trying to fix these broken systems but rather *are* we going to start. In the end, the only way to serve is one soul at a time."

Lou never met a guy named Alabama; Alabama was before his time. Dean Link knew Alabama well, because he was a constant presence at the Maranatha Temple. Nobody knew his real name. He wore a secondhand varsity letterman jacket that had ALABAMA emblazoned across the back, hence his street name. Although he had been through court-ordered detoxification twenty-one times, Alabama continued to show up at the Temple night after night in a drunken state.

Alabama was almost as good a racist as he was an alcoholic. He was well known for calling African Americans by names they did not appreciate. One night he hurled the n-word at a large, muscular black man who, as it happened, had also arrived at the Temple under the influence. The black man reacted by pulling out a knife. Alabama answered with his own knife. Dave came between the two drunks and issued an ultimatum.

"Look-it here," he commanded, his eyebrows forming an angry V. "I don't care what you guys do to each other outside of this building. But there will be no fighting in this establishment. Give me those knives."

Too stunned to do anything but comply, the men handed Dave their weapons.

As it happened, Alabama was one of the homeless men who transitioned from Maranatha to the new center as soon as it opened. As before, Alabama would arrive at the center intoxicated. Nothing, it seemed, was ever going to change Alabama.

One night at the center Dave spotted Alabama playing checkers with a Notre Dame volunteer, a young man who was in his sophomore year. Each time this student came to the center, he would seek out Alabama. They would play cards or checkers, and they would talk. The student's influence was such that Alabama entered into voluntary detoxification.

When Alabama returned from his twenty-second detoxification experience, he was a new man. Never again did he answer to that old nickname. He told people, "My name is Michael. Alabama died." Then he would tell them the date of Alabama's demise. It was the date that he had entered voluntary detox.

Michael stayed sober for the rest of his life. He got a job at a local fast-food restaurant. He moved into an apartment. He fell in love with a woman he met at the center, and she moved in with him. They were faithful in their common-law marriage until his death.

In his capacity as director of the center, Lou witnessed variations on this story over and over again. In his view, when a model like the one at the center is employed, success in helping people break the cycle of homelessness is not an unusual outcome. It is failure that is the surprise.

"The greatest challenge at a homeless center or a prison is the resuscitation of hope: helping people believe that there is some dignity in themselves, and that change is in fact possible for them," Lou says. "Many threw in the towel on themselves long ago. They had horrible things done to them in their childhood, and they've done horrible things to other people along the way. They cannot forgive, respect, or love themselves until we get them to a point where hope is resuscitated.

"If they don't have the kind of relationship where somebody believes in them, where somebody knows their name and cares about them, it doesn't matter what kind of programs you put together. Medical programs, mental health programs, job training programs, educational programs—none of that matters if you're not able to resuscitate hope.

"How do we resuscitate hope? First, by the environment. Whether a neighborhood, a homeless center, or a prison, it should be a place where people walk in and know that here is a place where people take pride. Second, by the way that we treat them. Third, by opportunity. Not only must we give them the opportunities to confront and address their weaknesses, failures, and needs; we must also create opportunities for them to express their giftedness. This is how they rediscover their self-esteem.

"Dave Link conceived of and birthed this 'baby.' I was privileged to nurture it through its infancy. But Dave is a visionary. He's a prophet. He looks to galvanize a community around a good idea. That good idea is always other-centered, and it's always God-centered. He's done this for the Law School, for the University of Notre Dame, Australia, for the homeless, and now he's doing the same thing in prison ministry. He's doing the same kind of thing for people who lose a beloved spouse. Like him, they can choose to convert their grief into a constructive force.

"Dave has never been limited by the place that he's in. He's always thinking more broadly. Father Hesburgh was the same way—he was much more than a university president. He used the university in the same way that Dave used the Law School: as a platform to impact the deepest challenges that we face as part of our human condition. And so in some ways it didn't matter what Dave was doing. In life service, in mission, it's not about job description. It's not about what you do in life. It's about how you do it.

"Dave's ethic of service . . . his spirit . . . his search for meaning and joy in all that he does—there is a golden thread that runs through all the apostolic placements that he's had over the years. And, really, the way he's done each of those jobs varies very little."

L ou left the Center for the Homeless in 1999 to begin his administrative career at Notre Dame. Drew Buscareno, ND '91, MS '96, was his successor, serving until 2003. Brian Connor served a one-year interim term until the center was able to entice Steve Camilleri, ND '94, to become executive director.

Steve, who began at the center in August 2004, has held true to the center's original mission statement and has expanded services during an economic downturn. From time to time, financial "angels" like actor and television personality Regis Philbin swoop in to assist. Regis, who graduated from Notre Dame in 1963 and whose daughter Joan was the last of more than four thousand students to be admitted to the Law School during Dean Link's deanship, is not shy about broadcasting his love for Notre Dame. Like many loyal Domers, Regis knows of and supports the

Center for the Homeless. During Steve's first year at the center, Regis brought his television show to the DeBartolo Performing Arts Center on the campus of Notre Dame and raised $75,000 in donations for the center. In Steve's fifth year as director, Regis lent his celebrity status and contagious enthusiasm to the center's twenty-four-hour dance marathon fund-raising event.

Walking through the sprawling complex, Steve greets and is greeted by everyone. Forty full-time and five part-time staff members as well as between three and four hundred volunteers help Steve make this the dynamic center for healing that it is. A tour of the center reveals that it is quite an operation.

Guests who hover near the receptionist's desk greet everyone who enters. Anxious to be helpful, they spring into action when citizens come through the doors lugging donations. A pleasant meet-and-greet room just off to the side features a wall of books and printed resources, with four-top tables and chairs grouped in front of it.

Controlled access to the residential area ensures the safety and security of guests. The residential facilities are divided into two main dormitories, one for men and the other for women. Single parents live with their children in family units. Steve explains that as residents progress through the center's programming they can gain greater privacy in transitional dormitory rooms shared with just one roommate or in off-site residential accommodations.

At every turn there is something to admire. Steve points out newly painted walls, work done by a former guest who graduated to independence two years earlier. Every room is clean and bright. The place looks fantastic.

Guests can relax, socialize, and watch television inside one of two lounges—again, one for men, the other for women. There is a family library, but books are also integrated throughout the center. There is a colorful playroom for the children. One entire wall is covered by an enchanting floor-to-ceiling mural depicting a sunglass-wearing dragon with his snout buried in the pages of an open book. Children can also play outside within a fenced courtyard, where durable child-size picnic tables and a small jungle gym await them. A room for middle schoolers provides a place for older children. Computers are available for use in the computer room. A small chapel provides a place for nondenominational worship.

The Montessori Academy is on the premises, the only Montessori school in the nation whose entire student roster comprises homeless or formerly homeless children. The children of parents who have been successful enough to leave and start a new life are welcome to continue the Montessori education they began while they lived at the center.

Next door to the Montessori classrooms is a nursery for infants. The center also boasts an on-site medical clinic where adults and children are treated. Guests with substance abuse problems receive treatment through the center's vigorous partnership with Madison Center, which is a hospital division service. The kitchen is overseen by an executive and a sous chef, both of whom are full-time employees. They are assisted by two part-time employees and by a constant flow of guests who learn by working in the kitchen. Meals, snacks, and coffee are enjoyed in a light-drenched café.

True to the beacon of light Dave had followed in the creation of the center, the various facets of the center represent the implementation of strategies designed to minimize the crippling effects of spatial mismatch.

Stepping from the building to the city sidewalks, Steve points to a landscape hangar and explains that there are as many as twenty guests who work in the landscaping crew. During the winter months, the crew performs snow removal; annually their labors produce $400,000 in revenue.

Emerging trends in homeless demographics called for a new type of expansion. Sadly, with a large number of people who served in the United States armed forces now homeless, a separate housing facility just for former servicemen was opened on Veteran's Day 2011. At the Robert L. Miller Sr. Veteran's Center, as many as twenty-five men can be helped at one time. Just like all the other guests, on the day they arrive the men are assigned a therapist and a coach. They receive treatment for medical issues, post-traumatic stress disorder (PTSD), and drug and alcohol addiction. Job training will help them reenter a society many have not participated in for years.

Just outside the Veteran's Center is a curious sight. Right smack in the middle of an impoverished inner-city neighborhood a beautiful garden is in full bloom. The garden was planted in a 65-by-150-foot parcel of land adjacent to the center, where the refuse of inner-city poverty had been accumulating for decades. Critics scoffed at the notion of a working garden. They predicted that the yard would be trashed just as soon as the evidence of urban blight could be removed. They were wrong.

On this summer day, Steve stands in dazzling sunlight and surveys a bounteous garden. Tomatoes are hanging thick on the vine. Melons, zucchini, and squash are resting on the harvesting table, ready to be brought into the kitchen. Sunflowers and purple coneflowers bloom in profusion. Butterflies, a symbol of transformation, skitter from blossom to blossom.

Steve explains, "First of all, we have transformed a harbor of blight, which benefits the city of South Bend. For our guests, this is a peaceful place of retreat. We also hold socials for staff and guests here. In the summer, acoustic musicians perform open-air concerts.

"We all need a purpose in life. This garden is important in that it gives many of our guests a purpose. They love working in the garden. It gives them a chance to know the feeling of making a valuable contribution. Every summer, flower cuttings are arranged in bouquets and then delivered to more than two hundred benefactors, simple but heartfelt expressions of gratitude. As many as ten thousand meals are produced from this little plot. Our guests plant the seedlings, nurture the crop, harvest the produce, and see the fruits of their labor in their meals, transformed into something beautiful and nourishing. They're seeing a productive cycle from start to finish, sometimes for the first time in their lives. We talk about breaking the cycle of homelessness. But this is a productive cycle we want them to see."

When it comes to homeless Americans, it's not a case of what we want to hear first, the good or the bad news; they are one and the same. It's good that the center is able to help an average of 1,200 people every year. It's good that the facility's capacity is 275 people on any given day. But the fact that the center is always filled to the maximum is also the bad news.

In the twenty-three years it has been in operation, the center has helped more than 51,000 human beings break the cycle of homelessness.

In 1947, before he became a published author, Jack Kerouac wrote a soul-baring letter to his friend Neal Cassady, the man who would become his muse for *On the Road.* In the letter, Kerouac confessed to a personal worldview that is reducible to one word: love. Speaking of the here and now, Kerouac observed, "Life must be rich and full of loving—it's no good otherwise, no good at all, for anyone." Kerouac then turned his eye toward eternity and wrote, "We will all die some day and it would be one hell of a joke if we all died in darkest ignorance of one another, oh brother my brother, what a travesty it would be, turned on ourselves."

Dave and Barb worked to dispel that "darkest ignorance of one another." They did not see cultural, racial, or social differences in the furrowed brows of the poor. They saw somebody's son. Somebody's daughter. Dave and Barb knew that behind the poverty of these people were inner beauty and untapped potential.

Fulfilled for many years by this kind of charitable work, Dave might have hit a plateau and stayed right there. He might have remained focused on the plight of the homeless. He could have taken up the cause of building holistic healing centers all over the country. Instead Barbara turned his attention to serving people who had even less to their names than the homeless.

PART THREE

COMPASSION

Prison as Crucible

D ave knew almost nothing about where the prisoners at Indiana State Prison had come from. He decided that he must learn all that he could about them and about their way of life. And so he walked the ranges.

Dave walked the ranges, and he met Alabama, after Alabama, after Alabama. He took it upon himself to be the person who sat down and opened up his heart to each of these people. For hours and hours, in hot weather and in cold, he walked from cell to cell, from pod to pod, and shared his life, experience, and knowledge. What made him unique was that he shared in *their* lives. He listened. Because Dave brought friendship based on reciprocity into their lives, many of these Alabamas were able to locate their inner Michaels.

In addition to roaming the ranges, Dave taught courses on justice, ethics, and the law. Christopher "Nick" Nicholson was one of his first students.

Nick, a member of the General Christian community, keeps a photo album with his belongings. In it are pictures of Nick in military uniform and cap and gown, family pictures of him with his parents, and pictures of Nick holding his little boy. Nick says that the story of why he is in prison begins when his son was two years old.

He was working full-time for Emge Packing Company in Anderson, Indiana, while attending night school at Ball State in Muncie. Nick, his wife, and their toddler lived with their parents so that little Matthew would be spared spending his days in childcare. One day Nick stopped home between work and night classes and leafed through the daily mail as his dad stood beside him at the kitchen table. In the pile was an envelope from the courthouse.

"What's this?" Nick wondered. "Did I get called for jury duty?"

Reading the letter out loud, *Now come ye forth . . . etc., etc.,* Nick was uncomprehending until he came to the phrase *dissolution of marriage.* He was stunned. Nick recalls that this letter was the first clue that the woman he loved wanted out.

He says that he turned to drugs and alcohol to deaden the pain, and that his life spiraled out of control. One night, in what he describes as a drug-induced coma capping off a two-week binge, he fell asleep in a cornfield. When he woke, he made his way to the house of a senior citizen who lived down the street and around the corner from his folks. Nick had done odd jobs for Maxine Heitger. From time to time, Maxine had lent him money, which he says he always repaid. He says that his intention on this particular night was to take enough money to finance a fix. He bound Maxine's arms and legs and put tape over her mouth. He says that he reassured her that he would telephone someone to come and help her. But after he left, Maxine suffocated.

Felony murder.

Now in his late forties, Nick says, "What would have made a difference was if I had encountered somebody like Doc *before*.

"Drugs took me down, but Doc—Doc and the Holy Spirit—changed my life. Now I know the truth about myself, and about God and the power that is available to me through the Holy Spirit. Before, I didn't have the power to say no. There was nothing to fill the voids in my life when I was hurting."

Once his mind and heart had been opened to the monstrous "other" he had once been, Nick emerged from a surreal inner world.

"One day Doc told me, 'Nick, you are a fine person,' and I was floored. '*You* are telling me this?' I asked in total disbelief. I had an epiphany, just sitting there with him. We prayed. I cried. What the Lord downloaded into me was that I was not alone anymore. He had sent an inspirational man who would help me and work with me."

Attendance at Dean Link's lectures was a kind of a crucible in which the residue of Nick's former self was fired, and in the process, his volatility was incinerated. Through dialoguing with the dean Nick's raging self-absorption was dissipated and his conscience was reborn. Dave, says Nick, was the catalyst he needed to set him on a new path.

Nick understands now that it's not all about Nick. "I learned from Doc that our circumstances don't change the callings of our lives." He says that he is always seeking ways to be helpful at Indiana State Prison. He believes that one way of helping is through serious study of the Bible. He uses his knowledge to promote nonviolence and to intervene in life-altering moments.

"The Word of God is quick and powerful. I've seen it. I've seen men come with the intention of doing harm, but when the Word was spoken, they couldn't. They couldn't because in my heart I stayed in that Love."

Nick says that he has learned through this experience how to submit and surrender to the Lord, and that he wakes up every day anxious to discover how God will use him. There is much that Nick does to atone. He serves his brothers in prison by participating as a mentor in a suicide-watch program. He says that Maxine came to him in a dream and told him, "I forgive you," so in her honor he has helped with the establishment of a Whole Wellness Program.

"This is a real church," he says. "But there are more than two thousand men here, and—I'm not certain, but I think that—by the numbers, we're supposed to have at least four full-time chaplains. We have never had anywhere near that number. And we have far too few chaplains like Father Dave. This situation creates a combustible environment. It's crucial to have religious programs. *Crucial.* This religious empowerment might be what keeps a man from killing someone. There is potential to do so much more for the men who live and breathe and want to know the sense of family that the church imparts."

In an effort to pick up the slack, Nick and others shoulder the responsibility of being available when a brother needs to vent. They listen, empathize, counsel with the Word, and pray with their brothers.

"I hope and pray that this situation has been created by God so that we will all come together, just like in the book of Acts."

As if to reassure himself, Nick opens his marked-up Bible

and goes straight to the book of Acts. He places his finger on a page and runs it along the lines of a passage as he reads. Nodding, he murmurs, "He'll make a way. Love will prevail in here."

Love has prevailed for Nick.

"I used to be afraid to love," he confesses. "Now, I'm afraid not to."

Now the Lord is the Spirit; and where the Spirit of the Lord is, there is liberty. —2 Corinthians 3:17

---

7. THE LEADERSHIP CRUCIBLE

There is a type of leader who does not ask to be placed in positions of leadership. Such people are quiet servants who do not seek nor do they have a need for the title of leader to be conferred upon them. Although the mantle of leadership is a cloak for which no pattern exists, and as such it cannot be reproduced, purchased, or inherited, instinctive leaders do not wrap themselves in this mantle so much as they discover that it has been laid upon their shoulders. The ability to lead is a gift.

This gift is bestowed on prophets who are of their times yet not of their times. They are people who operate within special dimensions of charisma, grace, and vision. Although no two leaders are alike, each has a potent combination of qualities that makes him identifiable, and leaders are more difficult to define than they are to recognize. So it is with one of the most significant figures in Dave's life, Father Ted Hesburgh.

Father Ted is an international leader. His particular constellation of gifts coalesced to create a savvy political animal. He has been on a first-name basis with an astonishing array of world figures. Across the globe, he has served the causes of peace, justice, civil rights, higher education, science, spirituality, and moral development.

But Father Ted is also the heartbeat of Notre Dame, and the campus bears witness to his influence. The Kroc Institute for International Peace Studies, for example, and the Kellogg Institute for International Studies both were natural outgrowths of Father Ted's efforts in the public sector, including his sixteen presidential appointments involving work on major social issues. In 1957 Dave noted with interest that President Dwight D. Eisenhower appointed Father Ted to be a charter member of the United States Commission on Civil Rights, and Dave followed Father Ted's career in civil rights with avid interest. Years later, Notre Dame's Center for Civil and Human Rights was born of the passion for justice shared by both President Hesburgh and Dean Link.

Impressive as these buildings are and important as their forums have been, there is a simple black-and-white picture that best embodies the spirit of Father Ted's leadership. The picture, taken by an unknown photographer at a rally held at Chicago's Soldier Field, shows President Hesburgh locked arm in arm with The Reverend Martin Luther King Jr. Considered by many to be a national treasure, the picture hangs in the permanent collection of the National Portrait Gallery. On the campus of Notre Dame, this image of solidarity is displayed in bustling LaFortune Student Center, because Father Ted belongs first and foremost to the students.

Father Ted is casual about how this iconic image came to be. He recalls that on Sunday, June 21, 1964, he was following the news coverage of the Senate's passage two days earlier of the Civil Rights Bill. Chicago stations reported that Dr. King would be speaking at the "Illinois Rally for Civil Rights" that afternoon. Father Ted was disappointed to learn that neither Mayor

Richard M. Daley nor His Eminence Albert Meyer, Archbishop of Chicago, would be present on the dais. Father Ted was resolute. Dr. King and the cause he was serving merited the support of the Church. From this place of moral certainty, Father Ted sprang into motion. Without a clue as to what he might find when he got there, Father Ted jumped into his Oldsmobile and drove to Chicago.

Once at Soldier Field, Father Ted waded through a crowd of some seventy thousand people. He and another priest spotted each other. Like Father Ted, this priest, a young man from Chicago, was compelled to attend the rally so that he would be a visible member of the Catholic Church participating in the fight for civil rights. The two priests gravitated toward one another and then stood side by side in the vast multitude. Father Ted shares what happened next.

"Martin was up on the platform getting ready to deliver his speech. He looked down and saw the two Roman collars in the crowd. He wanted to make sure that everybody was in his corner. He hadn't gotten anything from the Church, but when he saw the two priests down there, he figured, 'If I get them up here, I'll have the Church on my side.' So he had his aides bring us up onto the stage. I was on one side of Dr. King and the other priest was on the other side, with two Southern Baptist guys on each end. We stood there, locked arms, and sang 'We Shall Overcome.'

"Martin and I came from different backgrounds, but we had a common cause. Martin was coming at it from the standpoint of one of the suffering minorities, and I was doing it as a member of a commission established to obtain equal opportunities for all Americans. So the two fit exactly, and we could stand arm in arm and make it work. It was one of those instinctive actions that you don't plan; it just happened. It was no big deal. I just wanted to be present. It was just the right thing to do."

Although the leadership styles of Father Ted and Martin Luther King Jr. were different, the two men were simpatico, and both of them had been goaded into action by their principles. But the fact is, where others hesitate, leaders are already in motion. Leaders are casual about their accomplishments. For them, this really is no big deal.

When Father Ted invited Dave to become dean of the Law School, he spoke of a mission. He envisioned a school of law that would achieve an international presence with a reputation that would be earned by producing attorneys who would bring the highest ethical standards into positions of leadership in their communities. An essential precondition for the success of this mission was insight into purpose.

"Notre Dame takes a stand on Christian leadership," Father Ted explains. "That's important in that it gives us a grounding, and with that grounding we could become a law school that is different from those that just turn out good lawyers without worrying too much about the ethical background of lawyering.

"We have a great tradition of Christian law that goes back beyond the Middle Ages. It is strong and it is direct. We don't fudge on it. For a law to be good, it must be a *just* law. A just law must take into account the demands of human nature and its various manifestations. Whether we're talking about marriage or civil service or any kind of human activity, there is a law governing it. The law is wedded to justice as its ideal. *Lex iniusta non est lex,* or 'an unjust law is not a true law.'

"There are some people today who are lawyers, and they just manipulate the law to their own purposes, not the purposes of justice. They are stigmatized as being venal lawyers. Regretfully, there are plenty of them out there."

In Father Ted's view, the purpose of Notre Dame Law School was to educate attorneys-at-law who would embody, practice, and enforce the noblest ideals of justice. When Father Ted and David Link joined together, the result was a powerful force that made such goals achievable.

At a meeting in 2011 in Father Ted's beautiful office on the thirteenth floor of Notre Dame's Theodore M. Hesburgh Library, the two men talked about the Law School and about leadership.

"The secret of leadership," says Father Ted, "is that you must belong to something bigger than yourself.

"And then you have to say, 'How can I lead the power of this place to do good things rather than to either drift and do nothing or to just be neutral in everything?' "

"Whatever I know about leadership," says Father Dave, "I learned from you."

At the age of ninety-four, Father Ted could nod with satisfaction and direct right back at his protégé the credit that Dave tries to ascribe to his surrogate father.

"You did very well, David."

"We had fun, didn't we?"

"We did. And we built a *great* Catholic law school."

"I remember very well all the ways in which you reached out

to me when my father passed over. That was a very traumatic time in my life. And you became my father."

"Well, you were a great son, David, I'll say that."

It is a pleasant walk across the main campus from Father Ted's memorabilia-filled office to the Administration Building, where the president of the university and his assistants bend to their labors beneath the golden dome. There the Reverend James E. "Jim" McDonald, CSC, who from 2005 to 2011 served the university as associate vice president and counselor to President John I. Jenkins, CSC, was happy to recount his four years as one of Dave's associate deans.

Father McDonald, an attorney-at-law, first joined the Notre Dame faculty in 1997, handpicked by Dean Link to serve as associate dean for administration at the Law School. Father McDonald was responsible for what he calls the "nuts and bolts of running the Law School," responsibilities that included managing the operating budget and supervising the admissions office.

Dave had been dean for more than twenty years when Father McDonald climbed on board what Associate Dean Bill McLean often called "our happy ship." A Camelot-esque aura enveloped the Law School. Father McDonald was in a position to view Dave during the twilight years of his deanship, and he realized that he was watching a real pro in action.

"I listened to all of Dave's speeches when I was associate dean, and he was a great inspiration. His faculty and staff looked forward to one particular speech that he gave every year to the first-year law students. In it he described an encounter with someone he would refer to as 'a dean of a famous law school on the East Coast.' "

In his speech, Dean Link relayed an encounter in which this "other dean" boasted that he was building the Cadillac of the legal industry. Shrugging his shoulders and nodding, Dave added, as if it were an aside, "which, by the way, I believe to be true. His law school *is* producing the Cadillac of the legal industry. The good thing about Cadillacs is that you can trust that they have all been made to a standard set of specifications. Buyers are assured that they are purchasing a product of fine quality."

At about this point in the speech, many students were feeling confused. Why was their dean bragging about someone else's law school?

"But here at Notre Dame, we are building the Maserati of the legal industry."

Father McDonald recalls, "It was a line that the faculty and staff had heard over and over again, but we all waited for it with tremendous anticipation because it had such a powerful effect on the students."

Dean Link explained that Maserati had earned its superlative reputation for unmatched design and attention to detail because every car was hand finished. Each luxurious vehicle emerged from production having been appointed for one particular client. Then Dean Link welcomed his students into the land of the Maseratis.

The speech was important. It established the level of expectations for each of the sojourners who were beginning their three-year adventure on the high seas of USS *NDLS*. Dean Link delivered this speech to twenty-five incoming classes. Each and every time, he observed a remarkable phenomenon.

"From my podium," Dave says, "*I* saw *them* seeing themselves as individuals! Immediately, they responded to that concept of being unique, superlative, outstanding, handcrafted, different. Finer. They were *Maseratis*! I was alerting them to the idea that they were about to discover their own purpose in their professional lives. And they got it. This was the moment when they realized 'Hey, he's right! I haven't come here to be like anybody else! I have come here to be the best me that I can be.' Each time I gave that speech I was able to watch a remarkable phenomenon: the dawning of an identity. I could see it in their eyes."

Father McDonald smiles as he remembers that moment. "The first-year students had their eyes glued to Dean Link as he spoke, while our eyes were transfixed by the faces of the students. But the important point here is that not only did Dave believe it but it was true. There *is* a unique character to the Notre Dame Law School. And Dave embodied it in his own life."

Not everyone who is a great speaker is a great leader; nor is every great leader a great speaker. What may be more important than the ability to command the attention of a crowd is the ability to capture and hold the attention of one person. Father McDonald remembers that this was another of Dave's talents.

"Whomever Dave was talking to," he says, "that person was the center of his attention. It was as if no one else was in the room. Everybody knows that Dave is a great orator. But he was also a great listener. You could see that when he moved through the Law School. He talked with people, and it wasn't just shaking hands and slapping them on the back, saying, 'Hi, how are you?' He was really talking. He knew *everybody's* story. He was someone who really cared about what was happening to people in their lives. Clearly, even before he became a priest, he was a priest."

Father McDonald enjoyed Dave's leadership style because it gave him freedom to exercise his own judgment.

"Dave delegated a lot. He trusted in the people he hired. He gave them his vision, but then he let them do their work to help him to achieve that vision. The law always has these different . . . not factions, so much as different points of view—on how the law should work. But Dave was not an ideologue of any sort. He was a reconciler. He tried to keep these different groups together."

As dean, Dave established an open-door policy that started at the top. The door to his office was open at all times, except when there was a meeting that warranted privacy. He wanted students and faculty to feel as though they could drop in anytime. He also introduced biweekly, agenda-free, open-forum meetings with the students as a strategy for maintaining reciprocal lines of communication. At these Town Meetings, held in the student lounge on Fridays at noon, Dean Link and his students would gather in a convivial setting and discuss policy, air grievances, consider future directions the Law School might take, and explore rumors that circulated from time to time. Visiting professors were blown away by the courageous platform. Anyone could ask any question of the dean and they would receive a straight answer. Also impressive was the maturity, respect, and dignity displayed by the students, especially when they were in disagreement.

One memorable Town Meeting focused on the aftermath

of a tragedy. Driving home after having attended a Law School party and other celebrations at which beer had been served, a student had struck and killed a pedestrian. Dave was horrified. The accident caused him to consider, "Why do I have a building where any student can be served a beer?"

Rather than making decisions on policy from the pulpit of the dean's office, Dave brought the matter to the students in a Town Meeting. There he was able to get a read on the views of his student body. He told them that he was opening up a discussion out of his conviction that they should confront the issues as a community. He suggested that a refinement and restatement of the official stance on consumption of alcohol at Law School functions was in order. His students agreed.

Taking it to the next level, Dave challenged the students to form a committee, and he delegated that body the task of researching and articulating a policy that reflected the finest ideals of the entire community.

As it happened, the suggestions the student committee proposed were far tougher than the changes he would have made if he were working in an administrative vacuum. As a manager, he could have solved the problem. As a leader, he allowed his students to solve the problem.

The celebration of the birthday of Dr. Martin Luther King Jr. is of special significance to both Father Ted and Dave. In 1979 Notre Dame held a campus-wide celebration of Martin Luther King Jr. Day. Father Ted contacted Dave and told him that he wanted Dave to deliver the famous "I Have a Dream" speech.

"Father Ted," Dave said, "you may not have noticed, but I'm white."

Father Ted's response left no room for further discussion.

"You've got a great voice, Dave. We're going to do it in the church."

When Dave and Barbara arrived at the packed Basilica of the Sacred Heart, Dave was confident that he had prepared well for the event. He became a bit unnerved, however, when he spotted Martin Luther King Sr. seated in the front pew beside Father Ted. Dave felt not only the enormity of his responsibility but also the reverence of the moment. How could he do justice to this magnificent speech in the presence of the orator's father?

Assuming the lectern, Dave looked to Barbara. Strengthened by the smile on her face and encouraged by her eyes sparkling with excitement, Dave delivered a stirring rendition of Dr. King's speech.

After the event, someone snapped a picture of Martin Luther King Sr. standing with the Links on either side. In the picture, a broad smile lights the face of a jubilant "Daddy King," who has reached out and pulled the dean and his darling wife close to him. On Dave's face is a look of bewildered wonderment. But Barbara is as radiant as a bride.

At Indiana State Prison, other than religious worship, precious few events address the mental, emotional, or spiritual health of the prisoners. Martin Luther King Jr. Day happens to be one of those special occasions. In 2006, when several distinguished guests assembled at Indiana State Prison to honor the life and legacy of Dr. King, the chapel was jammed. This was a very big deal for all the residents.

Prisoner Larry Smith sat near the stage, observing the assemblage with interest. Cradled in his lap was his acoustic guitar that sports an image of a white peace dove on the front of the body and another that is inlaid on the head. Larry noted that Dr. Vernon G. Smith, Indiana state representative, and Governor Mitchell Elias "Mitch" Daniels Jr. were present, and he was impressed by the way they carried themselves. Even so, one man in particular stood out among the crowd.

"Wow," thought Larry. "That man. There's something about him. He's different."

That man, he would soon learn, was prison volunteer and seminarian David Link. As he watched, something stirred in Larry's heart. He sensed that this person was special. He had no inkling that he and the stranger would someday become friends.

Tall and spry, Larry seems to have dismantled the protective barrier surrounding his personal space. His ready smile, a rare thing behind The Wall, signifies approachability. His balding pate glints like a helmet beneath fluorescent tubes, but what is lacking on top is balanced by a silver Fu Manchu mustache and two lively eyebrows whose movements accentuate his expressive blue eyes.

"I'm just an old country boy," sixty-year-old Larry says with a shrug.

"When I came in here, I was not a nice person. I wasn't a very outgoing person, either. I was carrying around a lot of guilt for what I had done. But then I started writing gospel music."

At the Martin Luther King Day event Larry had been asked to perform "Your Grace Amazes Me," the first song he ever

July 12, 1958: High school sweethearts David Link, twenty-one, and Barbara Ann Winterhalter, twenty, are married in their hometown, Sandusky, Ohio.

Early 1960s: Lieutenant Commander Link, shown here as Lieutenant (Junior Grade), Judge Advocate General (JAG) Corps, with David, Mary, and Maureen Link.

1979: Martin Luther King, Sr. embraces Notre Dame Law School's Dean David Link and his wife following Dave's reenactment of Dr. Martin Luther King, Jr.'s "I Have A Dream" speech at the Basilica of the Sacred Heart at the University of Notre Dame.

1983: Dean Link competing in the Chicago Marathon. Against the odds, Dave was a serious runner for fifty years. Diagnosed with polio at the age of four, doctors told his parents that even if Dave were to walk again, he most certainly would never run.

1989: As founding president of the University of Notre Dame, Australia, Dave delivers his Inaugural Presidential Address. During the two and a half years it took to create the new University, Dave also continued his leadership of the Notre Dame Law School as Dean.

1994: After having mowed the grass, "Papa" gives one of fourteen grandchildren a ride on the tractor.

1996: Former President Jimmy Carter and Habitat for Humanity architect LeRoy S. Troyer with Dean Link at a project site in Vác, Hungary.

1998: The family gathers at Dave and Barb's fortieth wedding anniversary celebration. Encircling Barb and Dave, from left to right, are Teran, David, Maureen, Pato, and Mary.

At the Link residence in South Bend, Indiana, the wrap-around porch overlooks six wooded acres and the St. Joseph River. (PHOTO BY THE AUTHOR)

The chapel at Indiana State Prison. Constructed more than a century ago and designed for use as both a place of worship and as a theater, the 6,905 square-foot room seats 386. (PHOTO BY THE AUTHOR)

2010: Indiana State Prison resident David Parrish performs "Discovery Through the Ashes," a song he wrote about culpability and redemption on the "one-way train" of incarceration. (PHOTO BY THE AUTHOR)

2010: Indiana State Prison resident Bill Dixon reflects upon how different his life would have been if he had been blessed with a father like Dave Link. "Every time I see that man," he says, "it makes me want to be his son."

(PHOTO BY THE AUTHOR)

Easter, 2011: The Reverend David T. Link and Indiana State Prison resident Jeff Krumm prepare for the celebration of Mass. Father Dave is wearing the chasuble that inspired the Native name given him by Native American prisoners when they adopted him into their tribe. (PHOTO BY THE AUTHOR)

2011: One of the most significant figures in Father Dave's life is hero and surrogate father University of Notre Dame President Emeritus Reverend Theodore M. Hesburgh, C.S.C., who holds the world record for the most honorary degrees bestowed upon an individual and is the recipient of the Presidential Medal of Freedom as well as the United States Congressional Gold Medal. (PHOTO BY THE AUTHOR)

Former felon Gary Sparkman says, "Meeting Father Dave when I was incarcerated and becoming a success when I got out proves that God is still in the business of making miracles." (PHOTO BY THE AUTHOR)

Every day, Father Dave visits the grave site of the camerado to whom he was married for forty-five years. Barbara Link died of ovarian cancer on November 1, 2003. (PHOTO BY THE AUTHOR)

attempted to write. He was proud of it because it seemed to him that the lyrics had come from God Himself. As he recalls, "I woke up in the middle of the night and had these words on my heart. I had to get up and write them down."

> *Oh so many years ago,*
> *when I had so many dreams still ahead of me,*
> *all I ever wanted was to believe in someone*
> *and have someone believe in me.*

Larry strummed his guitar and sang of his aloneness before a standing-room-only crowd. His lyrics concluded with praise for the presence that had saved him from loneliness:

> *And then one day I found a friend*
> *who lived and died and rose again,*
> *and proved his love when he gave his life for me.*
> *Oh my God, your grace amazes me.*

At the conclusion of his performance, Larry was surprised to be called to the lectern by the gentleman who had captivated his interest since the beginning of the celebration. Dr. David Link complimented Larry on his song as well as his performance. Larry says that this was a life-changing moment.

"I was blown away. To be in the presence of those people and be *praised*! I didn't know how to respond! I had *never* been told that I had done *anything* good!"

Larry may spend the remainder of his life in prison, yet he marvels that a new role model came into his life.

"How can somebody who did what I did—I had *nothing* to offer society—how could I meet a man like Dr. Link? He is the *first* person who ever believed in me. He has helped me to have confidence in myself. We've developed a connection. I share everything with him. I look up to Dr. Link more than I look up to anyone.

"He made me understand: I may be in prison. But prison doesn't have to be in me."

Tolerance implies no lack of commitment to one's own beliefs. Rather it condemns the oppression or persecution of others.

—President John F. Kennedy

8. THE ETHICS CRUCIBLE

Ambition is a quality that has acquired negative connotations from its close kinship with ruthlessness. But there is a positive side to ambition, as seen in the way that people like Dave "push the envelope."

This expression has not always enjoyed widespread usage within the general population. It was first used in a technical and engineering context to refer to a mathematical envelope, which is something nonmathematicians might understand as the absolute boundaries of any and all possible solutions. In effect, these boundaries create an envelope in which all possible solutions to the problem are contained. The expression was pilfered by aviators, who adapted this concept for use in the fields of aviation and aeronautics. Here the envelope refers to the known limits, both upper and lower, of successful flight.

Early on in their marriage, Dave and Barb established that living with intensity was how they wished to go through life, and Dave's careers were distinguished by this attractive intensity, this positive side of ambition. He pushed the known boundaries because he refused to allow his dreams to be limited by them.

Dave learned from his father that men of honor wield

positions of influence within a certain code of conduct. This philosophy was deeply rooted in Dave's work ethic. "You keep your eye on the prize, yes," he says. "But you have to decide what the prize is. Is it my own advancement? Or is it the advancement of someone else?" One of the great legacies of Dave's deanship is that he conveyed this work ethic to his students.

Elton D. "EJ" Johnson earned his undergraduate degree from Florida State, where he was a football star. He came to Notre Dame Law School in 1998 fresh from National Football League tryouts. EJ served as vice president of Black Law Students Association. He participated in the International Law Program in London. And he was a driving force in helping to create a faculty-student basketball tournament that the students named the Dean Link Classic.

A special pregame contest kicked off the First Annual Dean Link Classic held early in 1999. Dave and EJ went one-on-one, playing to twenty-one. EJ spotted his dean twenty of those twenty-one points.

Spirited students crowded the basketball court inside Stepan Center. During warm-ups, the students were apparently so surprised that Dave was able to sink any baskets at all that, each time he did, great bursts of cheers erupted from the sidelines. At the end of the warm-up session, the balls were collected and put away. Faculty and student players retired to their respective benches. Dave and EJ moved to center circle.

The 290-pound NFL contender stood there in all his sleek, muscular, panther-like athleticism. He peered down from a six-foot-four vantage on his six-foot-nothing foe.

There was no tip-off. EJ handed Dean Link the ball, saying, "See what you can do."

Dave stunned his patronizing opponent with a quick run down the right side and a classic soft hook that sent the ball swishing through the net. The crowd went nuts.

"Illegal shot! Illegal shot!" shouted EJ. Turning to the now-riotous student section, he appealed for support. "He never left his feet! That's an illegal shot!"

Some yelled in agreement, "Yeah, that's right! You have to leave your feet!"

Dave seized the opportunity to turn the furor into a teaching moment.

"You may not have noticed, EJ, but I'm white, and everybody knows that white men can't jump."

After a protracted debate—these were, after all, lawyers and future lawyers—the shot was ruled legal.

EJ persuaded Dean Link to go one-on-one for another point.

Dave repeated the same play, and the shot was good. Again the crowd went wild.

"Dean, let's go again. Best two out of three."

"EJ, in that case, I've already won."

"Hm. That's true. Well, let's play one more point. Just one more."

The crowd was all for it, so Dave agreed. On this third and final point, Dave knew that EJ would not let him get away with going down the right side of the court as he had done twice already, so his strategy was to take the ball down the left side of the court. He successfully executed a crossover dribble but immediately afterward his knee hooked around EJ's leg. The next thing he knew he was on the floor, and he was in pain. Dave spent the rest of the evening in the emergency room with a meniscus tear that would plague him for the rest of his life.

Prior to this injury, Dave ran ten miles five mornings every week. One of his hobbies was participating in marathons and 10K races. The knee injury was so severe he was forced to give up his running routine. Getting in and out of his car and climbing stairs was tough. When he reached his seventies and found himself walking the ranges at Indiana State Prison, the pain was sometimes excruciating. But, in a crazy kind of way, he doesn't mind since it reminds him of EJ.

EJ is special to Father Dave not just because of the First Annual Dean Link Classic. More significant is the manner in which EJ passed a test of judgment and character in the Ethics class Dave taught to every first-year student.

It was Dave's tradition to begin discussions about representation of an unpopular client by introducing his class to a United States Supreme Court case that deals with the issue of freedom of assembly. The case, *National Socialist Party of America v. Village of Skokie* (432 U.S. 43 [1977]), is sometimes referred to as the Skokie Affair. Dean Link challenged his students to decide whether as practicing attorneys they would agree to represent the Nazi Party in a legal matter. He selected a student to represent each side of the dispute and then led the two in a debate about the merits of representation. Each year that he had taught this lesson there had been close to a fifty-fifty split on the hypothetical proposition, so Dave knew that this particular class session would be both lively and important.

In 1998 Dave looked directly across his desk at the intense, talented African American athlete who sat in the first row. Never one to shy from a challenge, Dean Link selected this student, EJ, to argue the position for representation. He conducted EJ through classic "unpopular client" scenarios. Each time EJ was consistent and right on target with his responses, asserting that he would represent even the most despicable clients.

Dave was impressed. Although it was obvious that EJ was struggling with his own personal opinions, it was also clear to the dean that EJ was thinking like an attorney. Dave decided that he could risk pushing this astute student even further.

"Okay, EJ," he said, taking a little stroll back and forth across the front of the classroom. "Let's go back to the original case. Except that now it is not the Nazi Party that wants to march through Skokie, Illinois. Instead, it is the Ku Klux Klan, and they want to march through South Bend and across the Notre Dame campus."

In 1924 a historic and riotous confrontation had indeed taken place between the Ku Klux Klan and Fighting Irish students.

Dean Link paused for effect, pivoted, and looked straight into EJ's eyes. "Would you represent the KKK?"

Beads of perspiration broke out across EJ's forehead. "Yes, sir, I would," he said.

"So that must mean that you believe in what the KKK preaches?"

Now standing and gripping the sides of the dean's desk, EJ answered through clenched teeth, "Of *course* I don't agree with the KKK, but I *do* believe in representation. I would represent."

"This is a civil case, EJ, so there is no constitutional right to representation."

"I *know* that, sir, but I think they have a *moral* right to representation. And so, while I have no respect for the KKK, I would represent."

Coming back to his desk, Dean Link challenged EJ one last time.

"Okay, EJ. Here is the final question and then you are off the hot seat. Let's say the Grand Dragon of the KKK comes to your office. He asks you to represent the Klan. He says, 'We don't care if you are a good lawyer or not. We just want a black man to represent us.' Would you represent?"

EJ leaned across the dean's desk and got right in Dave's face. In a stage whisper just loud enough for the dean to hear, he growled, *"Remind me to kick your ass sometime!"*

EJ straightened. Then, loud enough to be heard throughout the classroom, he delivered a principled response that was precisely what Dean Link was hoping to hear.

"No, I would not represent because now they are using me and my race for a cause I cannot support or be associated with. I would kick their butts out of my office."

These days EJ's curriculum vitae bears a strong resemblance to that of his dean. After earning his Juris Doctor, EJ established a private legal practice in South Bend. He is an adjunct professor at Brown Mackie College in South Bend, where he has been honored with the Outstanding Professor Award. He has devoted countless hours to organizations such as Big Brothers Big Sisters, Hope Rescue Mission, ChildServ, and the National Kidney Foundation. He has taught classes on racism at Brother Rice

High School in Chicago, and was awarded the St. Joseph Central Catholic Volunteer Award.

EJ says that it was not until he met Dean Link that he was awakened to the true meaning of compassion.

"Meeting Dean Link has been paramount in my life. He's so powerful and yet so gentle. When I think of Dean Link, I think of the Latin saying *res ipsa loquitur*, which means, *the thing speaks for itself*. He never blows his own trumpet. He does things for people and never looks for any return.

"Using his example, I've been able to target the skills that I have to motivate others to achieve an objective. Before I met him I didn't have that focus. He put the advancement of others in the spotlight and brought it to the forefront, and I learned from him that it's not just a feel-good thing; it's a duty. The things I learned from him, and the things that he did for me—I'll do them for someone else. Volunteering is my modus operandi. I try to perform the kinds of acts that I know he would be proud of."

In his practice, EJ handles many more pro bono cases than he should.

"I cannot turn away those who are powerless and voiceless any more than Dave Link could. I know I won't make any money on these cases. I see that. But I always remember what Dean Link said when I first met him. He talked about how Notre Dame Law School needed a more diverse population. He thought that Notre Dame law students should have a sense of what it is like to have come from a different place. A great percentage of the students hailed from a Catholic educational background—there were only four African American students in my incoming class. But Dean

Link wanted his students to be exposed to the reality that there are other people out there who are not as privileged. People for whom the journey has been very different. Though you may have no idea what it is like to be racially profiled or to live in a town where the Klan is active, there are those who do. By diversifying the student population, Dean Link offered the students opportunities to absorb the notion that less privileged people want the same kinds of things from life. Things like freedom, justice, and dignity. Dean Link inspired us to think about helping our neighbors. About using our professional talents and our status in the community to help someone who is underprivileged.

"Dave Link is someone I consider a true friend—a best friend. I have received counsel from him that I never received from my own father, counsel on everything, including relationship problems. He was a confessor long before he became a priest. The collar is just a uniform."

EJ says that it is easy for him to understand why Dave Link would eschew the ease of retirement for prison ministry. "He was dean of a top-twenty law school. But when he became a priest, Dave Link was fulfilling an even higher calling. The ultimate calling. Now he's doing things that go beyond our physical world. He's healing from the inside. This is spiritual healing."

Dean Link's view of the law as a healing profession has been the North Star by which EJ has navigated time and life. "In *every* class we discussed the ethical aspect. We always asked one question further, where we examined not just a law but also how it is applied to society, and *then* we asked, 'What is the virtuous thing to do in this situation?'

"We live in a society where almost everyone is driven toward making the almighty dollar. We have lost the concept of doing honorable and righteous things. What Dean Link embodies is that you can do both. You can make money but also keep your personal integrity while you conduct yourself with the highest ethics. Mortgage bank securities, derivatives, and hedging bets on things that are speculative—an ethical person would realize that this is not how you do business. Greed will always get you in trouble. These days, everyone going into a profession must approach their career having a sense of the importance of doing the right thing. That's what we learned at the place I think of as 'the Dean Link School of Ethical Law.'

"As dean, Dave was helping to equip future attorneys with the tools to go out and heal. I didn't nail that concept until I was practicing. It was then that I realized the brilliance of his vision. It sinks in when you agree to take a case and you see the relief on the faces of your clients; now they know they have someone who cares. Someone who will help solve their problem. It was during these kinds of moments that I realized that I have been given a gift. I am privileged to have a law degree. I will use this gift to make a living.

"But I will also use Dean Link's example. I will pass on what Dave Link gave to me.

"I'm a torchbearer. Dean Link handed me the torch."

A human being is a part of the whole called by us universe, a part limited in time and space. He experiences himself, his thoughts and feelings as something separated from the rest . . . a kind of optical delusion of his consciousness. This delusion is a kind of prison for us, restricting us to our personal desires and to affection for a few persons nearest to us. Our task must be to free ourselves from this prison by widening our circle of compassion to embrace all living creatures and the whole of nature in its beauty.   —Albert Einstein

9. THE COMPASSION CRUCIBLE

The spiritual leader of the Native American community at Indiana State Prison is a man known by most as Bear. Bear Hayes was assigned to work as a chapel clerk during the two and a half years that Dave was attending seminary. Bear recalls, "I remember when Dave was coming back and forth from seminary training in Wisconsin. One day he came into the office, sat down, and asked me what we need the most. I told him that we need an advocate. Since then he has been our advocate in more ways than you can imagine—that word times ten."

Dave saw in Bear a well-organized, loyal worker. Bear saw in Dave a good man. On the day that Bear got married, Dave's status was elevated to best man.

On October 10, 2008, Chief Standing Bear Hayes, Turtle Clan Chief, Eastern United Lenape Nation, was joined in holy matrimony with the Reverend Tricia L. Teater, a Buddhist priest, a hospice caregiver, and an artist.

Father Dave has been in attendance at other prison weddings. Some are unions between two people who seem to genuinely care about each other, but many are marriages of convenience or obligation. Often a generic celebrant whose primary concern seems to be whether the marriage license is in order races through a minimalistic ceremony that is devoid of personality and emotion. The brevity and businesslike coldness suggest that these weddings have been deemed uninteresting and these unions, insignificant. Bear and Tricia's wedding was different.

Father Dave was waiting in the lobby for Tricia's arrival. She came breezing into the prison flanked on one side by her sister and on the other side by her friend and fellow Buddhist priest Roshi Diane Martin.

Father Dave smiles as he recalls his first sight of Bear's bride.

"She was beautifully dressed. She wore an Indian-style suit made of golden brocade. She looked gorgeous. Absolutely gorgeous. And she was *so* excited."

There was to be a Native American ceremony followed by a Buddhist ceremony. The Native circle was already gathered and in place as Father Dave and the three women were clearing security, slipping off their shoes to display the soles of their feet and getting patted down. Finally, the animated bride and her wedding party sailed through the lobby door. When they turned a corner Tricia's heart leaped to see her groom just ahead, poised and expectant and looking right at her with a smile on his face and smiles in his eyes. Just as any fellow marine would have done, Bear made sure that his shirt had been starched until it crackled and that there was a crisp crease running down the front of his khaki trousers.

The wedding was held in the Hoosier Room, which is one of the more dignified corners of the prison. Located across the corridor from the security booth where volunteers temporarily surrender their driver's licenses, the Hoosier Room is the prison's Switzerland. Neither behind The Wall nor outside, it is a place of relative neutrality where prisoners sometimes meet with people as when, for example, they talk with high school students or civic groups about life in prison.

It was a small affair, as are all prison weddings. Bride and groom are allowed to invite just one guest each, and the two guests do double duty as legal witnesses. Father Dave stood beside Bear, a man for whom he has great respect, a man he calls "friend," and felt as if he were a member of Bear and Tricia's family. Roshi Diane conducted the Buddhist ceremony, personalizing it so that it reflected the spirituality and bravery of two unusual people. As Bear and Tricia exchanged the vows they had written, Father Dave was awed at the transformative radiance he saw on their faces. At seventy-two years of age, Father Dave had been to a lot of weddings in his life, but this one stood apart. In a flash of insight, Father Dave understood why. "Bear and Tricia have forgotten where they are," he thought. "They are in a prison. But they have gone somewhere far beyond imprisonment. And where they are physically doesn't matter to them at all." Father Dave felt unworthy of standing so close to love this rare, idealistic, and electrifying.

Tricia had been coming to the prison for years. She had developed a deep connection to the Buddhist community at Indiana

State Prison and loved the work she was doing as a volunteer chaplain. She also had served as spiritual advisor to Donald Ray Wallace Jr., who was executed in March 2005, as well as to Wallace's family. The experience was so emotionally grueling that afterward Tricia requested a leave of absence from her prison ministry.

Throughout the years of serving the Buddhist community as a volunteer prison chaplain, Tricia sometimes heard Bear giving teachings to his Native American brothers. She was impressed with Bear's gifts as a teacher as well as by his spirituality. One morning she was enchanted by sweet, sweet music she heard coming from the other side of the chapel. It was Bear playing his flute.

Once a week Native Americans gather to worship and uphold their ancestors' traditions. Cedar, sage, and sweet grass are burned. In the Native tradition, the prayers of the worshippers are carried upward to the Creator on a pathway blazed by the smoke trails, which has the further purpose of creating a 'corridor' or opening by which the Creator's blessings can come down upon each one of them. The men sing songs in the Lakota language and receive a teaching from Bear.

Bear sculpts his teachings like Father Dave shapes his homilies. In each teaching Bear shines a light on the human condition in the hope that his brothers can use the lesson to find and fulfill their life's purpose. At one of his teaching sessions Bear began by acknowledging that life in prison is difficult, sometimes intolerably so. But he exhorted his brothers to change their point of view about hardships.

"Too often," he said, "we lose sight of just how much we have to be grateful for. And we must be grateful for our hardships. We must be more thankful for the hard days than we are for the days that are not as difficult. We should feel more gratitude since the hard days are our opportunities."

He pointed out the wisdom of viewing challenge as an opportunity. He said that everyone should welcome suffering as a chance to shine for the Creator. To suffer, he contends, is to burnish and refine the love that is inside our souls. Bear cited the power of prayer as a tool to help people through this process of refinement.

"Prayer is the greatest thing. Prayer can give meaning to our lives. Even in this place, prayer can give meaning to our lives. Prayer can change each one of us. And prayer can change the course of the world."

Teachings like these piqued Tricia's interest in Native spirituality even as they revealed Bear's goodness. At the same time, Bear was intrigued by what he was learning about Buddhism. Soon they discovered that beneath their outward differences was a bedrock of intense spirituality. Finally they sat down and confessed, each to the other, that they were having feelings for each other.

Prison rules forbid volunteering when there are personal connections to prisoners. Although she dreaded the consequences, Bear and Tricia agreed that the ethics of the situation were clear. She was stricken at the thought of abandoning her beloved Buddhist community. She couldn't imagine giving up the ministry and teaching she was doing as a prison chaplain. She was inconsolable that she would no longer be able to be in the same room as Bear, to sit beside him or hear his teachings or be captivated by the dreamlike lyricism of an ethereal flute wafting from somewhere over there.

Yet none of this was worth having if it meant sacrificing honor and truth.

Although she was already on a leave of absence, Tricia immediately resigned her position as volunteer chaplain.

Father Dave watched as Bear underwent a startling metamorphosis.

"I saw a real conversion. Bear went from being a tough prisoner to being a model prisoner. All of the anger dissolved. He changed into someone who is always helping others, always counseling someone in need."

Bear gives credit for his transformation to Father Dave and to his wife. "Doc inspires me to be loving and compassionate to everybody regardless of who they are," he says. "He inspires me to want to be the best person I can be. I love Doc. I'd do anything in the world for him. I've never met anyone like him.

"I know that he loves his wife dearly to this day. I feel the same way about my wife. When I met my wife, she softened me. I think she's a lot like Doc's late wife. She doesn't try to change me; she just influences me by her example."

One way that Father Dave advocated for Native American prisoners was by supporting their request to bring the custom of Inipi into the prison. Holy and sacred, Inipi is as essential to Native Americans as the Bible is to Christians, the Torah is to Jews, and the Eucharist to Catholics. Inipi is a purification ceremony that is held inside a domed hut, where Native Americans sit on the ground around a pit filled with heated rocks. Water is poured over the rocks, and the hut fills with steam. Native songs and prayers emphasize the purpose of the ceremony, which is to purify and cleanse both the body and the mind. It is a time-honored tradition that has its own exacting rules of etiquette. The Inipi is protected from defilement by its practitioners, who ensure that untruths are not spoken nor are bad deeds performed during this sacred ceremony.

For Bear, leading his clan is especially difficult since there is no sweat lodge at Indiana State Prison. Bear explains, "For the Native American traditionalist practitioner, participation in ceremony is vital to the overall well-being of the individual, not only the spiritual well-being but in all areas—physically, emotionally, and socially. It is the foundation upon which our connection to the Creator, our ancestors, the community, and the world around us is built. Without it we are lost."

Studies and experience have shown that without the kind of spiritual connection Bear is talking about, most prisoners are lost. More than two million Americans are presently incarcerated. The greatest percentage of prisoners are African Americans. Despite constituting the smallest ethnic segment in the country, Native Americans make up the second-greatest percentage of prisoners. The third highest percentage of prisoners are Latinos. No matter what the ethnic heritage or religious affiliation of an inmate, there is no doubt that faith-based prison programming and the development of spirituality informs, reforms, and completes the moral maturation of people who were and continue to be involved in crime and violence.

Indiana State Prison Superintendent William K. "Bill"

Wilson, who was appointed in March 2010, believes that religion and religious opportunities are essential to every corrections operation.

"I don't know that we have any other aspect of corrections that is more important to managing our population than religion," says Superintendent Wilson. "Chaplains and religious volunteers are true believers in what they're doing, and that is especially true about Father Link, who is effecting change in a grassroots movement. He's truly here to try to improve the lives of those who have been less fortunate and to help them find something of value in their lives. Religious and education opportunities are crucial to the corrections mission."

At Indiana State Prison a large sign that reads BUT FOR THE GRACE OF GOD hangs on the back wall of the chapel. Father Dave says that every time he looks at that sign he is reminded that but for the grace of God he too could be dressed in prison khakis.

There are those who point out that these people did something awful and they deserve to be in prison, and Father Dave does not dispute this point. Researchers estimate that between 15 and 35 percent of all prisoners are true psychopaths. Neuroscientists tell us that psychopaths do not care because they cannot care. Their brain structures differ in an organic way from the brains of human beings who empathize—people who understand pain and the consequences of their behaviors, people who have a conscience. Add a negative environment to this structural difference, and a dangerous psychopath can be created. Yet these dysfunctional, psychopathic prisoners need and deserve treatment, because to ignore the problem is not just inhumane; it is also costly for and perilous to society.

Superintendent Wilson observes, "Offenders can be very narcissistic—it's really all about them—and it's even worse in this environment because they have no one else to worry about other than themselves. We try to talk to the offenders all the time and tell them that if you have a personal issue, chances are that there are more of you that have that same personal issue, and so let's address the problem globally. When we do this, we hope to start getting them to think in terms of community versus individual needs. Once we can do that, then we have opportunities to start moving the culture forward so that they understand that effecting change can be done by a group more effectively than by individuals.

"However, we have to first of all recognize who wants that kind of self-improvement and who doesn't. I've got 365 offenders who are segregated from the rest of the population because they're not motivated yet. They haven't found some value that keeps them from making bad choices. And they may never be able to."

Father Dave agrees. "I'm not a 'Pollyanna' about the prison population. I'm not trying to say that these people didn't do something wrong. Are they better off here than with their gangs? Yes, in many instances. But still I ask, 'Why them and not me?'

"I have had a different experience as a citizen in America than most of these people have had. I know that I was lucky to have been mentored by truly great people of impeccable standards all throughout my life, beginning with my father and mother. It is true that God allowed the parents, relatives, siblings, neighbors, teachers, and acquaintances who have affected the lives of these men to operate with the gift of free will. These men, in turn, made decisions out of their own free will, and in many instances, those decisions landed them in this place.

"But there are many, many prisoners—people like Bear— who mature emotionally and spiritually during their time behind razor wire.

"Many of these men have made stupid mistakes. But once they have found God and if they are no longer a threat to society, why do we keep them in here?

"If I were running a prison, I'd see Bear as a great asset to the prison. But leaving him in here is a waste of taxpayers' money. It's wasteful not just in terms of what is being spent to keep him in here but also in terms of what society is losing by not having Bear on the outside."

In February 1998 Richard V. "Dickie" Taylor was convicted of murder by criminal recklessness and was sentenced to sixty years in prison. Dickie has changed in essential ways since then. "Dickie has turned his life around," says Father Dave. "It began with him coming to grips with and feeling deep remorse for what he has done. He shared a lot with me and was very emotionally involved in reviewing what has happened in his life. There were times when he broke down and cried. He said that he had come over to Jesus and that he wished he had done this before he got into trouble.

"Not only is he sorry for what he did, but Dickie has also decided that the best way to make up for it is by becoming a spiritual leader. He knows now that he has a job to do. He has a purpose in life, which is to help his fellow prisoners with their own spiritual journeys. He serves on suicide watch. He gives a lot of individual counseling, and he is not afraid to share in an honest way. He talks about his old life in contrast to his new life. He has come to me with questions such as 'How can I help this guy with such and such?' or 'How would you handle this type of situation?'"

Like many of the prisoners, Dickie understands that there is little chance he will be released from prison. Yet he tries to think about his life as if he were on the outside. He lives, as much as is possible within the prison environment, with purpose and dignity. He understands that his thoughts and behaviors are the stewards of his soul. From this perspective, Dickie talks about prisons in general.

"We underutilize the resources of the men in here who have changed," he says. "We also cut off the relationship with society. Men can't re-enter and be positive people unless there is a connection to society prior to release. We have to learn the societal norms. But even if we are able to gain education in the facility during extensive sentences, if we are never given the form to exercise what we've learned in here, then it's all for naught. We have to be able to utilize what we learn in whatever environment we're in—starting with in here. We need an outlet to give back and to express creativity—even in here. It's important—the link to society—it's so important.

"There are men here who want to express remorse. The victims here, as well as out there, are often in lower socioeconomic levels, and they don't trust. They don't trust the system. They don't trust medical or psychological services as a direct result of the system failing them so many times before. So they've picked up a stigma that they can't admit that they need help; they can't go over and ask for help. It's a brick wall that you can't burst through."

At forty-five years old Dickie, whose skin is the color of burnt sienna, has been at Indiana State Prison for sixteen years. He was there when Dave Link first started lecturing the lifers. He has come to know and admire Father Dave in the years since.

"One thing I can say: Father Dave *is* what most Christians talk about being. For me personally, Father Dave has been salvation—not the eternal life salvation but the everyday salvation that most of us need in here. Out of the dire circumstances of our lives, there is a brick wall, and it is right there. No one else can burst through it. Somehow, from the other side, that brick wall began to crumble. For me it was Father Dave who crumbled that brick wall. And then he helped me to get on over to the other side. Now, *I* done that—*I* had the choice of whether to cross to that threshold or not. But Father Dave crumbled my brick wall and helped me get on over. God used him as a vessel of salvation for me."

An annual tradition that was always near and dear to the hearts of Indiana State Prison residents was Family Day, the one day of the year that family members were able to sit and talk with one another. Dickie approached Father Dave at Family Day.

"Father Dave," he said, "I'd like you to meet my mother."

Turning to his mother, Dickie said, "Mom, I would like to introduce you to my brother by another mother."

Just as he had done at all of the academic functions he attended as dean of the Law School, Dave turned his full attention to the woman to whom he had just been introduced.

Dickie gets emotional talking about that afternoon.

"Father Dave comforted my mother. That is the greatest thing that he could have done for me."

Dickie has seen some acts of cruelty and retribution in his years behind bars, things he cannot risk exposing, but he says that what he has learned from Father Dave has made destructive impulses toward backlash disappear.

The word "punish" comes from the Greek *poine* and Latin *poena*. Both are words for revenge. One can see that these are also the roots of the English "pain." Punishment, then, is the deliberate infliction of pain and degradation. Long ago teachers took switches to schoolchildren they wished to dominate and restrain, or rapped knuckles and pulled ears to punish children for giving wrong answers. Dunce caps were used as tools of humiliation and ridicule. Today we know better. Science has shown that punishment and degradation are ineffective.

Punishment is a powerful deterrent to learning, to socialization, to maturation, and to growth. An overwhelming body of evidence reveals that punishment is the most potent stimulus of more violence. In other words, violence begets violence. If we want to create a violent person, all we need do is ensure that the person's life is characterized by two conditions. First, the person must be subjected to shame and humiliation. Second, the feeling of guilt in this person must be destroyed, and we do that by inflicting punishment that is both severe and continuous over a long period of time.

On the other hand, the most effective strategy for conditioning desirable behavior is positive reinforcement and positive role modeling. In his prison ministry, as he has traveled from one Indiana correctional institution to another, Father Dave has looked for but was unable to find a cohesive and effective program for positive reinforcement.

"One of the most critical flaws in the prison system," he says, "is the absence of a proactive system of rewards. Some residents reform while in prison. Many assume helpful responsibilities. Others become model prisoners. Some have put their own lives at risk to save prison guards in times of danger. These men are heroes. Yet there is no system in place that acknowledges, rewards, or offers positive reinforcement to those who do mature into better citizens."

Superintendent Wilson says, "We try to offer an environment in which there is give-and-take. What can I give an offender to help him improve without compromising the safety and security of the facility? But there is a fine line there because we don't have a lot of opportunities to reward the offenders for good behavior or self-improvement."

As the national crisis of over-incarceration continues unabated, Superintendent Wilson observes, "As a society we need to diminish the numbers of incarcerated offenders. We also need to do a better job of incarcerating offenders. To have offenders who don't pay child support, and drug dealers, and people who committed crimes while they were on drugs all incarcerated together makes no sense. The guy who is trafficking in drugs needs to be put behind bars. But the drug abuser needs treatment. He doesn't need to be put behind bars with the guy who supplied him with drugs. And then the guy who doesn't pay child support, how does he fit into that equation with either of those two? He doesn't need treatment; he needs a job. Yet we incarcerate them all as a group and tell the Department of Corrections, 'Here, you fix them.' We are being asked to meet all the deficiencies of what we did not do in our communities."

F ather Dave began to imagine reforming the system in such a way that prisoners could earn extra commissary and/or reduce their sentences. Certain that such a step would go a long way toward heightening safety in prison, he also believes that it would improve the effectiveness of the stated corrections mission. It would enhance the quality of life for staff and inmates alike. He began to conceive of ways that proactive rewards could be added into a system that is very good at reactive punishment. Proactive rewards would reverse the trend toward higher violence in the prison population and, at the same time, arrest the plummeting in morale of those who are paid to guard the prisoners.

He toured prisons in other states that have systems of positive reinforcement as well as transformative programming. These facilities are not run on the "lock 'em up and throw away the key" philosophy. Instead they make use of the time that people spend in corrections to turn their lives around. In Louisiana, for example, at maximum-security Angola, there is a two-pronged strategy that was implemented by Senior Warden Burl Cain: purposeful work—all of the inmates have a job—coupled with increased opportunities for spirituality. Cain's pioneering Angola Bible College has received much of the credit for a 70 percent reduction in inmate violence. In Texas, maximum-security Darrington Penitentiary followed the Angola model in creating its own transformative program. Prisoners who feel a calling to minister to their incarcerated brethren can enroll in the on-site, nondenominational Darrington Penetentiary Seminary. They have full access to an accredited theological library as they work their way through a four-year program and earn a Bible studies degree. The program is staffed by volunteers and supported by private grants and donations, so it incurs no cost to taxpayers.

The reforming approach that is followed at Angola and Darrington replaces negative thought patterns with positive ones. One of the intended objectives is to make better parents out of imprisoned fathers and mothers. This far-sighted objective is driven by the sobering statistic that between seven and eight out of every ten children of imprisoned parents will end up behind bars.

Positive reinforcement and proactive programming just make good sense. As Dickie puts it, "The key is that we have to be able to transform negative habits into positive habits. We have to learn how not to get caught up in our emotions. We have to get practice in telling ourselves *Things don't move me; I move things.* My identity crisis that I had previously? I no longer have that. My identity now is that I have been called on to be the expressed identity of God. But no matter what, we can't just throw people away."

Father Dave realized that putting together a workable plan to identify those prisoners who should be returned to free society was something that he could do—in fact, it was something that he should do. So late in the evening after the day's work was done, Father Dave began immersing himself in a body of literature on poverty, racial prejudice, and the prison empire. His readings showed him that poverty is an epidemic that has swept across our country just as smallpox once swept across continents and changed the course of history by decimating entire segments of the population. In recent decades, as victims of poverty became too numerous to be contained in ghettos, slums, and reservations, an elaborate political-social system was concocted and crowned with the euphemistic title of the War on Crime. Sociologists, criminologists, psychologists, economists, social justice activists, and clergy in every denomination have decried this war as the new Jim Crow and an ineffectual reaction to failures in our systems, including family, education, employment, and housing.

Father Dave questioned whether it was enough to continue ministering one-on-one to his brothers or whether he owed them something more. Was he being called to synthesize his previous careers—indeed, his whole life? Had God called him to prison ministry so that he could put together a comprehensive plan that would end the madness? A plan that would solve problems on both sides of The Wall?

He began puzzling out a program by which prisons and communities can assess prisoners who are ready to be an asset to society. For starters, removing prisoners from incarceration when they are capable of being productive members of society would provide massive savings to taxpayers. Night after night, Father Dave bent over his computer working out the details. He didn't stop until he had hammered out a ten-point Crime Peace Plan addressing the most vexing problems in the criminal justice system.

Father Dave's Crime Peace Plan outlines ways in which proactivity can be implemented within the prisons. Father Dave also recommends ways in which professionals and citizens can work together to bring more healing into society. One specific proposal suggests the creation of early-release review boards that would exist in cities and towns in just the same way that a board of education exists to reflect and uphold community-wide standards. These early-release boards would be designed to play an integral role in helping courts and prison administrators decide whether certain prisoners are good candidates for early release. Father Dave's Crime Peace Plan also endorses the adoption of measures that will help justice to be better served. One change to the present system recommends that all prosecutors be appointed rather than elected.

Father Dave gathered with a small group of like-minded businessmen with similar concerns about the overincarceration problem in America. Together they worked on creating employment opportunities for former felons and for military veterans. Father Dave connected with professionals who have experience with the implementation of life-changing programming in prisons.

Everything was starting to come together.

PART FOUR

CLARITY

But the father said to his servants, "Bring out the best robe and put it on him, and put a ring on his hand and sandals on his feet. And bring the fatted calf here and kill it, and let us eat and be merry; for this my son was dead and is alive again; he was lost and is found."

—Luke 15:22–24

Prison as Clarifier

The teaching of the washing of the feet was so important to Dave that it would be depicted on the first liturgical vestment he donned as a newly ordained priest. Knowing that Dave has always been drawn to the customs and heritage of Native Americans, siblings Dody, Bud, and Frank had located two Navaho women in Arizona who designed and hand sewed the white vestment. The front is replete with Native American imagery. On the back, a cascade of water stitched in silver metallic thread glitters in the light.

The Mass at which the sacrament of Holy Orders is administered is considered to be a new priest's first Mass, even though the presiding bishop is the one who is performing *in persona Christi capitis*. To distinguish the ordination ceremony from a priest's debut as celebrant, the first solo liturgy is known as a Mass of Thanksgiving. Dave had planned for not one but three Masses of Thanksgiving, and the first would take place the day after his

ordination. This Mass of Thanksgiving was celebrated in the Basilica of the Sacred Heart in the heart of the Notre Dame campus
on his fiftieth reunion weekend. One week later Father Dave celebrated his second Mass of Thanksgiving at Little Flower Catholic Church, the parish to which Barbara and Dave had belonged
all the years they lived in South Bend. His third Mass of Thanksgiving took place inside the chapel at Indiana State Prison.

Native American David Parrish was plugging in his guitar
in preparation for playing liturgical music when Father
Dave entered the chapel dressed as a priest. David's eyes swept
over the white chasuble with its symbols rich in Native American
meaning, and he was moved.

David has been blessed with the kind of youthful good looks
that belie his chronological age. His is the kind of shy, sweet face
that school photographers always seat in the front row of the el-
ementary class picture. His smiles are fleeting but worth waiting
for, and looking into his eyes takes courage. They are tunnels
that lead you to places where you must confront eons of suffering. An observer by nature, he has had countless opportunities to
observe Father Dave in action.

"I do not consider myself a Christian," says David. "I don't
believe in anything that man has made—the dogma. But I believe in the love and word of Christ, which I have merged with
my Native American belief, and I trust in people who live by
what Christ taught. And I trust Father Dave. Being a priest isn't
what makes Father Dave the way he is—it's being a man of God."

Not long after Father Dave's Mass of Thanksgiving at the

prison, David dreamed a powerful dream, which he shared with the Native American community.

"In this dream," he told his Native brothers, "I was living several hundred years ago, with Native people. Out of the woods and into the clearing walked two men wearing black robes. They were shot with arrows. I was observing this with no emotional content or reaction. In the dream, I wasn't feeling whether that was right or wrong.

"Then into the clearing came a man wearing a white robe. I saw that it was Father Dave. He was wearing that first robe that he wore as a priest; it is a robe that was made by two Navajo women. And I said, 'HOLD YOUR FIRE! HE'S A WHITE ROBE!'

"When I yelled, 'WHITE ROBE,' everyone stopped. They understood immediately. And they received him."

The Native American brothers decided that this dream was a sign. They conducted a special service in honor of the priest. The men adopted him into their tribe and, as a sacred offering, christened him with a new name.

A Native name.

White Robe.

When Father Dave goes behind The Wall at Indiana State Prison, he cannot help but believe that he is participating in the reenactment of an ancient teaching. He feels as if his love for these men is a language that is being communicated to God's prodigal sons. It is calling them to walk the path that will lead them home, where Love is the fire in the hearth that will warm their hurting hearts.

God is getting through to these woebegone sons, but He is not doing it alone. He is making use of one who delights in the law of the Lord. At Indiana State Prison, those whose lives have been touched by Reverend David Link believe that He has sent into that godforsaken place His very best robe.

The Lord is near to those who have a broken heart . . .

—Psalms 34:18

10. THE PRIEST THING

Dave's love for the men who lived behind The Wall rescued him from a black abyss of sorrow after ovarian cancer took Barbara from Dave on November 1, All Saints' Day, 2003.

All of the pallbearers who carried her casket to its final resting place in Cedar Grove Cemetery were women. Though it broke her heart to bury her dearest friend, Nancy Shaffer was one of them. With her fingers wrapped around the cool brass railing, memories of an elegant but understated friend who never gossiped nor stood in judgment of others filtered through Nancy's mind. She recalled the ways that Barbara had cared for so many people—strangers, family members, friends, anyone, everyone. Remembering a classic Barbara-ism, she smiled. In May of 1983, Dave and Barb were leaving for Florida, where Barb would undergo delicate brain surgery to remove a large acoustic neuroma. Brigid Dutile had asked if she could do anything to help in Barbara's absence. It was clear from her expression that Barbara was grateful for the offer. "Oh, yes, thank you, Brigid. Would you please be sure that the recycling gets put out on Tuesday?"

After Barb died, the Links' children feared that they would lose their father as well as their mother, so profound was his grief. He felt incomplete and directionless without Barbara by his side. She had always been his compass rose. Her passing seemed to demagnetize his life, and he had no clue which way to turn. With his mind stuck in an endless feedback loop of memories, it was a struggle for him to understand the meaning of her death. Clarity came when he was able to discern the meaning of her life.

Dave had always wondered where Barbara's prophetic progressiveness had come from. Way before the plight of the homeless hit the national radar screen Barbara was helping the poor on a daily basis. Dave was in awe of her quiet brilliance and wondered how someone as understated as Barbara could have been as influential as she was during her life. He knew that he had been living with someone who was gifted in the art of compassion. Not long after he was ordained, his grief was reconciled when he came to the understanding that Barbara had been used here on earth as an instrument of healing, and that by bringing her home, God seemed to be suggesting that she would be even more effective as an inspirational guide from her new vantage point.

Father Dave explains, "Our relationship has changed. Our partnership has not. I went from having a good partner to having an even better one.

"A moral compass comes from the grace of God. It is offered to all of us. We determine with our own free will whether to accept or refuse the gift. I am so lucky to have a partner who shares the same orientation toward justice. Barbara and I worked well together. But I can honestly say that we still do."

Even though home is an empty nest, when the Native American residents at Indiana State Prison bestowed on Father Dave the title of Honorary Native American, or when prisoners present him with poems they write about the effect that he has had on their lives, Dave feels as though Barbara is right there, sharing in everything that happens to him.

"Does she know? No question. She knows."

After Barbara was laid to rest, Nancy and Tom were aching as their friend seemed to gasp for air in a deflated, Barbara-less world. That he would find a new purpose in his career as a priest was astonishing. Virtually all of Dave's former colleagues and students confess that they were stunned to hear that Dean Link had become a priest. And yet, they reflect, it was predictable.

Tom says, "I think he found his way to the priesthood through the prisoners."

Jim Dahl admits, "The priest thing didn't make any sense until I heard about the prison thing. Then it all made sense."

Father Jim McDonald sees a continuity in all of Dave's incarnations. "When I arrived at the Law School, the stories were legendary of Dean Link reaching out to people who were suffering in some way. But throughout his entire life, there has been a consistency of focus that moves from one sphere to another. He worked for the homeless. He worked for the Law School. Now he's a priest, and he's working for prisoners and the criminal justice system. They all hold together in a concern for people who are in difficult straits. Even before, when Barbara was alive, he had the same concerns as he has now. He is all of one character."

Father Dave confesses that he is perpetually astonished that he is a priest. He says that catching a glimpse in the mirror of a man in a clerical collar never fails to startle him. Nevertheless, the greatest surprise of this anti-retirement is how much he loves his new career.

"I am astounded at the passion I feel for what I am doing and at the strength of my devotion to the team—the team meaning the residents of the prisons and myself. I never imagined this as a career move for me. But here I am. How did I get here? There wasn't a moment, or an epiphany, so much as a slow dawning over a period of time. I know now that this is my calling, but to be honest, I feel unworthy of doing it."

Dave completed seminary studies at the Sacred Heart School of Theology in Hales Corners, Wisconsin, zooming through a five-year course of study in two and a half years. He received the sacrament of Holy Orders from the Most Reverend Bishop Dale J. Melczek on Saturday, June 7, 2008, at Holy Angels Cathedral in Gary, Indiana. At seventy-one, he was older than the combined ages of the other two new priests.

Bishop Melczek explains that although his great love is the liturgy, he believes that one cannot separate the Mass from the recognition of the face of Christ in the poor, so he has established a strong diocesan commitment to serving Christ by serving the needy. For the bishop, then, "The ground was fertile for the gift that David brings. I feel indebted to him for extending my own personal ministry to those who are in most difficult circumstances, those who need the compassion of the Lord. I believe that if Jesus Christ came to earth today, He would be involved in prison ministry, just like Dave."

As Tom Shaffer had learned from his work helping students defend death row prisoners in the 1960s, "There is no work more dispiriting than working for prisoners. I believe that Dave can do this work because he is not doing it as a lawyer. If you do this work as a priest, you see your work through the prism of hope. Dave's faith is what gives him the strength to struggle through this most discouraging work."

Father Dave's assignment as a newly ordained priest was to minister to the incarcerated as deputy director of religious services and community activities for the Indiana Department of Corrections. He took vows of obedience and celibacy even as he maintained unbreakable bonds to his old life. He would always be Dad to his kids; he would always be Papa to his grandchildren.

Bringing love and an outstretched hand to the less fortunate has fulfilled Father Dave's career-long desire to help people attain their own life's purpose. More than anything, however, his prison ministry represents the capstone of Father Dave's guiding philosophy:

> *Who we are and what we have accomplished in our lives is not what will be discussed when we pass from life to afterlife. What will matter most of all are how many others we bring along with us to the gates of heaven.*

By learning what lies on the other side of the gates of a prison, Father Dave closed the loop on his legal education. Going behind The Wall inspired him to probe the matter of his own culpability. In self-reflection, he was forced to ask, "How does justice look from this side, with your attorney eyes?"

He also completed what might be called a doctoral in compassion, for he has learned the flip side of names and titles. His eyes have been opened to what it is like for people to have names and titles that are a disservice to them. The men at Indiana State Prison know this bitter truth all too well. They are aware of having been negatively impacted by their ancestral name, the troublesome baggage that comes with it, and the negative legacies that brought them here. "Would I be here, in this place, had I been born into the Link family?" they ask. When they talk about Father Dave, they say, "If only I had met him—or someone like him . . ."

Gary "Mo" Moore was skeptical when Father Dave first started coming to Indiana State Prison. He says that there have been other chaplains who have been less than honest with his brothers and with him. In time, Mo would decide that Dave was different.

"He's a great, great man. He's for everybody here, not just the Catholics, not just the Christians. He doesn't care what color you are. By him coming to us and being honest with us, we have more energy and more fellowship. When people have problems they can go and talk to him, and it relieves a lot of people out here who are stressed. He is a blessing. I just wish we had more like him."

In his capacity of deputy director of religious services and community activities, Father Dave put in more than fifty hours every week serving eight of Indiana's twenty adult prison facilities. He was on call twenty-four hours a day. He could be at the prison within minutes to counsel, give a blessing, or administer last rites in the event that there was violence, death, or suicide. He walked the ranges day after day, always getting a kick out of the call that would echo down the line whenever he entered a cell house. The first guy to notice him would act as the sentinel. "Our chaplain is on deck!" he would shout, and all profanity was ceased.

Father Dave loved presiding over Mass, but he was a constant presence at other religious services as well. His flock includes men who embrace twelve different religious denominations: Asatru, Buddhist, Catholic, General Christian, Eastern Orthodox Catholic, House of Yahweh, Jehovah's Witness, Jewish, Moorish Science Temples of America, Muslim, Native American, and Wiccan congregations. He also ministers to a thirteenth "congregation" whose members eschew membership in any faith persuasion.

"Although I am ordained in a particular religion," says Father Dave, "my mission in prisons involves healing human weaknesses no matter what belief systems are held by those incarcerated persons. My job, as I see it, is to encourage the least, bring hope to the last, search for a path for the lost, and offer friendship to the lonely."

One day at Westville Correctional Facility, a medium-security prison, Father Dave found himself giving counsel to a man who was almost inconsolable with grief. Another prisoner had asked if the man was related to a particular person who shared his last name. Nodding, the man answered, "Yes, why do you ask?" The first prisoner handed over the obituary section, which is how the man sobbing in Chaplain Link's office had learned of his mother's death.

Tears coursed down his face as this man struggled with regret. Less than one year was remaining in his sentence. He had been sustained during incarceration by fantasies of what it would be like when he got out of prison. He would be a new person. Someone his mother could be proud of. He was crushed that she did not live to see him a free man.

Father Dave asked a few questions about his mother. The floodgates were opened. One memory led to another. Soon the prisoner was drawing word portraits of his entire extended family. The personalities of aunts and uncles and cousins came alive, making it seem almost as if they were crowding their way into the tiny office.

Father Dave went home feeling unusually drained. He was unable to shake this emotional session from his thoughts. He rewound the mental tape recorder and replayed the scene over and over again. Finally, the meaning of the time that they had spent together became clear. It had been a virtual wake. During the time he had spent with Father Dave, a grieving son had eulogized his mother.

Father Dave was consoled. This was at least something. This brother still had a long way to go to get through the process of grieving, but at least he had taken the first step toward healing with a camerado at his side.

Father Dave has been an athlete and sports fan all his life. As a priest, he has found ways to use his avocations in counseling people, for instance, employing sports analogies to convey life-changing messages. One in particular is a favorite among the prisoners.

"We all start out with our names written in heaven," Father Dave tells them, "and only we can destroy that. But we know from the world of sports that every game of consequence is won in the second half. Well, this is your second half, my friend, and you are playing for very high stakes. You are playing for eternity."

This message can be transformative. In June 2012, for example, three men were plotting to take an officer hostage. A fourth, a man with a well-deserved reputation as a tough guy, intervened. He took the weapons the three had intended to use in the attack and delivered them to the on-duty major. Astonished, the major asked where the prisoner had gotten the weapons. Tough Guy said that he had found them on Main Street. Knowing how valuable these weapons would have been if Tough Guy had chosen to sell them, the major asked him why he was turning them in. The prisoner replied, "Because I was saved last night." Tough Guy had crossed over from agnosticism to belief less than twenty-four hours earlier.

Father Dave talks straight with the prisoners. His hope is that his words will spark chain reactions in a kind of reversal of the Irish blessing *May God hold you in the palm of His hand.* By using language that is meaningful to them, he can bring God out of the heavens—the heavens that can seem very remote to men who never see the moon—and into the reality of prison life. Now God is close, close enough for them to feel as if they can hold Him in their hands.

On July 29, 2012, for example, one of the Scripture readings described the feeding of the five thousand. The homily Father Dave prepared was titled "Man Up."

After the readings, Father Dave approached the lectern, plucked the microphone from its stand, walked into the space between the altar and the first row of seats, and became a moving target.

"You have just heard the story of how Jesus taught the five thousand followers. Then out of compassion the teacher performed an extraordinary miracle so that everyone could be fed.

"Today, I'm not going to feed you—I will leave that to Aramark and the commissary. I'm not even going to try to teach you. Once you have decided who you are, you can choose what you want to be and teach yourself what you should do.

"Here is a story that will show you what I mean.

"A man walks into a pet store. Near the entrance is a talking parrot. The parrot looks at the customer and squawks, 'Man, you sure are ugly. You are so ugly, you can trick-or-treat without a mask. You are so ugly, Ripley's *Believe It or Not* sent back your picture. They just could not believe it.'

"From his perch on a stool at the cash register, the proprietor apologizes profusely and tells the man that his purchase will be on the house. Then the proprietor comes out from behind the counter to give the bird a scolding.

" 'You can't talk to my customers like that! You do that again and I'll come back here, pull out all your feathers, and sell you to a company that makes dog food.'

"The proprietor returns to the cash counter, bags up the merchandise, apologizes, and promises that it will not happen again. The customer heads for the door. Although he is determined to avoid making eye contact as he passes the cage, he cannot help stealing a quick glance at the brightly colored bird.

"The parrot mutters, 'You know what you are.' "

Father Dave looks around at all the faces of these men whom he loves.

"I ask each and every resident in this facility: What are you? Are you a boy or are you a man? God created you as a boy but gave you the potential to be a man. Saint Paul tells us, 'When I was a child, I used to talk like a child, think like a child, reason as a child; when I became a man, I put aside those childish things.' Can we do that?

"My friends, being a man is not about how big you are or how tough you are or how many people fear you. It's not about how many tattoos you have or how many sexual encounters you have had. Being a man depends on whether you can put away the things of a child. Whether you are strong enough to give up lying, scamming, and manipulating. Whether you can give up the alcohol and the drugs, the dirty jokes and the cussin', fightin', and other childish habits you are holding on to.

"You are a man when you try to be the man God created you to be.

"Our Native American brothers tell us that we have two natures and that they are like two wolves fighting inside each of us. One of those natures is evil, the other is good. The one that wins is the one that we feed.

"Be the man who rises above it all. Be the man who chooses Jesus the Christ as a role model. Be the son you were created to be. If you are married, be the husband you were created to be. If you have children, be the father you should be. Be a real leader.

"Feed the good in you."

Father Dave has been looking rather fierce. His face softens. He smiles his upside-down smile and his eyes crinkle at the corners as he says, "May the Spirit guide you."

In October 2010, journalist Brittany Morehouse visited Indiana State Prison. A group of prisoners sat and talked with her about how Father Dave has changed their lives.

David Hoernig was the first to volunteer his thoughts. "I'm sixty years old. I did eighteen years then was out for eight years. My problem was that I hadn't dealt with what caused me to have my problems in the first place. I was stuck in denial. I realized when I came back here that, being my age and being sentenced to a hundred years, I'd never see freedom again. But Father Dave says that we always have eternity to look forward to. He says that it's never too late; we always have God. We have our eternal future to look forward to. This can be the beginning and not the end. It's kind of like a seed that has to die and fall to the ground in order for it to grow. My life isn't what I wanted it to be, but now it's in preparation for a new life."

Larry Edwards, the musician who met Father Dave at the Martin Luther King Jr. celebration, has been at Indiana State Prison since 1975. Larry talks about what a breath of fresh air Dave has been from his very first visit. "The atmosphere has been a whole lot more wholesome since Dr. Link started coming. He's altruistic, and that's rare around here. He remembers your name—that's a big thing—and he recalls things you talked about together even months later.

"He has so much compassion for people when they're hurting. I've had a number of death notices since I've been here. Other chaplains might leave your death notice with a shift supervisor and let them tell you instead of walking over to your cell to tell you themselves. But not Dr. Link. He reaches inside you and brings out a lot of things that you didn't know were there, and then you remember that they meant a lot to you. He's just chatting with me, and I'm driven with all this pain, but he pulls out little happy moments to think about. And I feel like I'm talking to one of my family members."

Sixty-two-year-old James P. Harrison, PhD, carries 250 pounds on his five-foot-two frame. His gray sweatshirt pools at his wrists but fits snug around his middle. His salt-and-pepper hair is close-cropped, his trimmed beard professorial. Anywhere but here he would look like a department store Santa Claus on his way to the gym. He is referred to by the prisoners as "one of the lucky ones," because after having spent more than eighteen years on death row, James's sentence was commuted and he is able to attend Mass and interact with members of the general prison population. It was while he was on death row that James earned his PhD, and he is proud of his accomplishment. He reminds the journalist several times, "That's Doctor Harrison. Don't forget to put in the 'Doctor.' "

James says, "Father Dave changes my reality, because he makes me know that someone cares. Me? I'm never gonna get out of here. When you lose your family, you've lost just about everything. But Father Dave helps us understand that our faith is our family."

James says that what keeps him going are his religious beliefs and the hope that he can help someone else. "We all could make a difference if we just add our own little bit. Then you get it all together and you have a better world. But it takes everybody to make up the whole."

When asked what his "little bit" might be, James knits his eyebrows together and considers the question.

"Just to listen," he says at last. "I try to listen to what the guys have to say and understand what they are feeling. And I try to comfort them."

Around the room, heads are nodding.

Gregarious David Landrum volunteers, "In here, there is a dark, negative tide pool all around us. But in this dark lake of phoniness, Father Dave is for real. He believes in what he preaches. He is sincere. And he is a good example to follow. For me, he's like a phone call home. He has given me a stronger belief. He has changed my prayer life. He inspires me to help others. He is making a difference in my life and in the lives of countless others. I feel as though the Holy Spirit sent him to us to let us know that somebody cares." Shaking his head, David Landrum concludes, "I wish I would have met him before I got into trouble."

Nick Nicholson adds, "This prison can be such a lonely and desperate place. There is a spirit of heaviness that seeks to envelop and depress all of us inside. However, God told us through His prophet Isaiah, 'I've given you the garment of Praise for the spirit of heaviness' (61:3), and He sent us Doc to show us how to wear it. As a result, many of us here are experiencing true freedom for the first time in our lives.

"There are no lost causes. There is some God in all of us. And sometimes the end of one life can be the beginning of another."

David Parrish has been listening attentively. Aware that he is the only one who has not yet answered, Brittany looks into his brown, soulful eyes. The unanswered question hangs in the air.

"Has Father Dave changed your life?" she asks.

David meets her gaze. With quiet conviction, he lays the question to rest.

"He's completed mine."

Fathers and friends are significant pieces in the vast puzzle that is life. Without them, the puzzle is incomplete.

Now Jesus sat opposite the treasury and saw how the people put money into the treasury. And many who were rich put in much. Then one poor widow came and threw in two mites [the smallest of coins], which make a quadrans. So He called His disciples to Himself and said to them, "Assuredly, I say to you that this poor widow has put in more than all those who have given to the treasury; for they all put in out of their abundance, but she out of her poverty put in all that she had, her whole livelihood." —Mark 12:41–44

---

11. GIFTS

P risoners who need to confide in Father Dave find their way to a tiny office located behind the stage in the chapel at Indiana State Prison. It is just a nugget of a room. Father Dave donated religious books from his own library to help fill the bookshelves in the room. He hung inspirational quotes and pictures on the walls, scrounged a couple of decent chairs, and the room acquired a quality of serenity. It has been dubbed the Peace Room. Here men examine their lives sometimes in confession, sometimes under the umbrella of friendship. Father Dave says that he listens, passes everything on to the Holy Spirit, and waits for a response.

He sometimes feels as though he is challenged to counsel under difficult circumstances. His best efforts often seem insufficient and small in comparison with the enormity of the need. One day, for example, a man who was locked up in the psychiatric ward requested a visit from Father Dave.

A prisoner who is confined to the psychiatric ward is isolated and not permitted to have newspapers, books, music, or television. Human interactions are kept to a minimum. It is not surprising that these people do not always make a lot of sense, or that one seldom knows how much of what one is saying is actually getting through.

When Father Dave arrived at this particular prisoner's cell, he found a man who was speaking gibberish. Every utterance was indecipherable nonsense. Even so, Father Dave stood there for quite a while. He hoped that his presence in and of itself would be enough to give this person some measure of comfort.

When it was time to go, Father Dave was astonished when the prisoner made a coherent request. He asked that Father Dave lead him in praying the Lord's Prayer.

The prisoner knelt on the cement floor. He reached through the steel bars so that he and Father Dave could join hands. He bowed his head and poured forth a heartfelt and flawless recitation of the Lord's Prayer, the most passionate that Father Dave had ever heard.

Minutes earlier, the man's mind seemed as if it were gone.

The prayer revealed that there was still someone in there.

Father Dave had gone but a few steps from that prisoner's cell when another prisoner called out from around the corner. "Hey—hey you! Could you talk with me, too?"

"Of course I can," Father Dave replied, and walked over to the cell. "What would you like to talk about?"

"I don't know. I guess anything is good."

So Father Dave talked about love. When the prisoner expressed doubt that anyone could love him, Father Dave talked about the all-forgiving love of God the Father. He chatted with this lonely, hurting soul for half an hour or more.

Afterward the prisoner insisted on presenting Father Dave with a gift.

Father Dave was startled. "Gift?" he thought. "How could this man have anything to give?" Meanwhile, the prisoner was rustling around in his cell. Shuffling back, he reached through the steel grid and placed a small plastic bag into Father Dave's hands.

"Take this," he said.

Inside the baggie were two halves of a graham cracker.

Father Dave's heart pounded with recognition.

"Thank you . . . thank you very much," he murmured. "But I can't take these. This is your dessert . . . this is your treat . . ."

"You came here and you talked with me. You prayed with me. I want to thank you. Please. Take it."

That night Father Dave sat at home staring at a framed poem that hangs on a wall.

> *God sends each person into this world*
> *with a special message to deliver,*
> *with a special song to sing for others,*
> *with a special act of love to bestow.*
> *No one else can speak my message*
> *or sing my song*
> *or offer my act of love.*

—JOHN POWELL, FROM Through
Seasons of the Heart

The baggie of graham crackers lay on the table beside his chair. Curlicues of steam rose from a mug of tea. Dave sank into a reverie.

I believe that everyone is placed here on earth for a particular purpose. It is not for me to know or guess at anyone else's purpose. That is a discovery to be made by them. All I can do is help them in fulfilling their purpose. For years I did what I could to help dressed in a shirt and tie and, now, with this collar that has given me a different kind of credibility. These men know that they can trust me. And it feels so good. I love what I am doing. Tonight, although I am tired, I am also elated.

But I wonder: Why do so few people care?

The whole thing seemed so out of tune. It wasn't just the prisoners. Everyone in the place was suffering. Morale was low even for the staff. At the information desk during a shift change, he overheard one officer talking to another. "If there was any other job in Northern Indiana," she said, "I'd be gone." The other replied, "I'd be right behind you."

It is not unusual for cell houses to be staffed by people who are not trained in clinical psychology. Some of them want to help but others are just paper pushers. One day, for example, Father Dave received word that he would have to give a prisoner living in D Cell House, a lockdown unit, notice that his daughter had died. Father Dave took the notice to the cell house. He asked the sergeant to bring the man from his cell to the office of the counselor for that living unit; then he sat down to await the prisoner's arrival. The living unit counselor, who is someone who has been hired by the state to be an on-site mental health counselor, was seated at his desk.

The prisoner was led into the office. Father Dave introduced himself. "I am very sorry," he said, "but I have some terrible news. We have just received word that your daughter has passed away."

The prisoner's reaction was oddly reserved, as if he had heard but did not truly comprehend.

"Would you like to talk with your mother?" Father Dave asked.

The man nodded. Father Dave picked up the phone and called the prison operator. He read her the telephone number so that she could dial out.

The prisoner spoke up. "Father, that is not my mother's phone number. That's not even her area code."

Father Dave checked the paper he was holding in his hands.

"That's what's on this paper."

"May I see?"

Father Dave handed him the page.

"Oh. This explains it. This is a guy who has the same name as me. We live in the same cell house but we've never met."

Father Dave apologized for the distress the institutional mix-up had caused, and the sergeant escorted the prisoner back to his cell. Soon he returned with the other prisoner. Again Father Dave, himself a father of daughters, had to look another man in the face and tell him that his daughter was dead at the age of four.

This father collapsed to the floor in a sobbing heap. He buried his face in his hands. "Oh, no. I can't believe this," he sobbed. "Oh, no. Oh, no. I can't believe this."

The entire time that Father Dave was speaking with both of the prisoners—the man whose daughter was still alive and the other father who was shattered by the news of his daughter's death—the prison counselor said not one word. He sat and stared at some papers on the desk, as if they mattered, as if they were of some consequence, as if they were important.

A few days before his visit to the psych ward, Father Dave had met in the Peace Room with a prisoner new to Indiana State Prison. Born and raised in Gary, Indiana, the new inmate had led a rough life. At twenty-two he was already the father of four. Even so, there was a childlike sense of wonderment about him.

The prisoner came to talk with Father Dave about his dream of sponsoring a South American child. It would cost $22 a month, he said, and he needed help in making that happen. He fantasized that when he got out, he would take his kids to Cancún, to the Bahamas, and to South America, where all of them would be able to meet this child he wanted to sponsor.

There was a break in the conversation. The prisoner looked around appreciatively.

"Are these all religion books?" he asked.

Father Dave nodded.

"Any of 'em have lots of pictures?"

Shepherding his thoughts back to the here and now, Father Dave picked up the baggie and cradled the two graham crackers in his palm. He decided that he would use them in tomorrow's homily.

On Saturday, December 4, 2010, as Father Dave wheeled his car into the parking lot at Little Flower Catholic Church, letters scrolling on the outdoor digital marquee seemed to wink at him, and he smiled. He had presented the sign to Little Flower as a tribute to Barbara.

Plows had shaped the previous week's snowfall into mounds. Scattered all over the parking lot, they looked like gigantic frosted gumdrops. After parking, Father Dave gathered his chasuble, Sacramentary, and briefcase from the trunk of his car. With one arm laden, he used the other to pull the church door open and stepped inside to a place that felt like home. Behind him the door sighed as it glided shut.

He glanced at his watch. He was plenty early. Good. He needed a little time to settle down. Even after all the years in academe, his stomach still fluttered every time he spoke to a crowd. He was especially revved up this morning. The homily he had prepared was so personal, it was important that he get it right.

He dressed in the purple vestments of the Advent season. He walked into the empty chapel and tucked his notes and a visual aid into the shelf beneath the lectern. He went into the hallway to greet the worshippers who were beginning to arrive.

The Scripture readings of the day from the Gospel of Matthew focused on Jesus and compassion. Father Dave chose one line—*Freely you have received, freely give.*—as the central idea of his homily.

With less than three weeks until Christmas, parishioners came to Mass feeling the stresses of shopping, baking, and family obligations. Once they seated themselves, however, they were offered a soothing view of a feathery snowfall through petite windows chiseled into the chapel's sandstone walls. It was as if the landscape, like holiday cookies pulled from hot ovens, was being dusted with confectioner's sugar. The congregants sang two enthusiastic, albeit off-key, verses of the processional hymn "Ave Maria."

Father Dave gave the opening blessing. He extended his arms and said, "Greetings, my sisters and brothers." He looked around the room, his face shining with happiness. He was delighted to be in this place, at this moment, with these friends. He dropped his arms, clasped his hands together, and gave a preliminary sketch of what was on his mind. "As we prepare for the celebration of the birth of our Lord and Savior Jesus Christ, we are surrounded on all sides by talk of gifts. Our mailboxes are stuffed with catalogues. Our televisions bombard us with images of gifts they claim will bring happiness to our loved ones. Today's Scripture speaks to us about gifts and gift giving.

"As many of you know, God has blessed me with an abundance of gifts. In fact, I may have been born with a silver spoon, but now I can honestly say that I've been gifted with a complete collection of sterling silver place settings."

A collective chuckle signaled that he had their attention.

"To begin with, I was given the gift of family. I was raised in a warm and loving home by parents who were outstanding in every way. I was blessed with wonderful siblings. I was educated at the finest Catholic institution in the world. I was married to a woman who was an absolute saint, and she did her best to raise me up to her saintly standards. That she never succeeded is not to be counted against her."

He moved in closer.

"I have been gifted in all these ways and many more—privileges and people too vast to number—and yet these do not begin to approach the enormity of one particular gift I have been given.

"We hear a lot of talk about the 'Good News,' but how many people think about what the News *is*?

"The Good News is all about the greatest gift that has ever been given! Given to us by God the Father, our greatest gift is Jesus, His only begotten and most beloved Son, whose life was sacrificed so that we might be freed from sin and know eternal life. As if that weren't great enough, the Holy Spirit has ensured that the loving sacrifice Jesus made for us is a gift perpetually given through the Eucharist.

"Later on we will read what God has to say about gifts and what He has to say about giving.

"And I will tell you about one very special gift that I received from a most unlikely giver."

During his homily he shared the story of the prisoner who had insisted on giving him a gift. He had brought the plastic baggie with him, and when the time came, he pulled out the two graham crackers, which he had come to think of as two mites, from the shelf beneath the lectern. He held them up for everyone to see and told them about the man who had given them to him as a gift of gratitude.

Perhaps he could get everyone in the chapel thinking about the abundance with which they had been blessed and about how they might share these blessings with their less fortunate sisters and brothers.

Blessed is the man who walks not in the counsel of the ungodly,
nor stands in the path of sinners,
nor sits in the seat of the scornful;
but his delight is in the law of the Lord,
and in His law he meditates day and night.
He shall be like a tree planted by the rivers of water,
that brings forth its fruit in its season,
whose leaf also shall not wither;
and whatever he does shall prosper.

—Psalms 1:1–3

---

12. That Missing Link

It is sometimes difficult to redirect one's gaze to look up instead of down, or ahead instead of to the past. Despair cannot be replaced by hope in one magical instant. Someone or something must bridge the abyss between those two states of being. For many people, David Link has been that bridge. Inside maximum-, medium-, and minimum-security facilities, he helps people cross over into new ways of thinking and new ways of living.

The Indiana Department of Correction has established a re-entry initiative known as PLUS (Purposeful Living Units Serve). During the last sixteen to eighteen months of a prisoner's sentence, PLUS programming addresses issues as varied as interpersonal relationships, religious diversity, anger and conflict management, the effect of crime on victims, and substance abuse.

Father Dave has taught several different PLUS classes at Indiana State Prison as well as at the South Bend Work Release Facility. The Work Release Facility, which is located in an impoverished area of downtown South Bend, has the capacity to sleep 108 prisoners at any given time. Prisoners live in dormitory housing units and are confined to the facility unless they have secured work outside the prison, in which case they are escorted to and from their jobs by staff.

Father Dave's students are crazy about him. All he has to do is step into the building and before he can climb a few stairs up into the vestibule they are encircling him to shake his hand, give him fist bumps, or envelope him in bear hugs. If he could be there every night, every one of his sessions would be overflowing with students.

Sean Bell was a student in Father Dave's parenting class. "I asked for his help because me and my girlfriend were having difficulties," Sean says. "Because of me being locked up and us being separated, there are some troubles and issues between us. We have to deal with these issues though, and we needed a mediator, and we found one in Father Link.

"In the old Western movies, remember Gene Autry, the cowboy in the white hat? That's who Father Link is. He's someone you just don't find no more. He's honest. If I'm doing something wrong, he'll tell me, straight-out, and then I try harder. He inspires me to do better."

It's been a long road to re-entry for Sean, a journey that has taken him in and out of prison in a series of incarcerations. He battles an overwhelming past every day of his life. He gets pensive when he talks about his childhood.

"My dad, Bob Bell, was a kind, loving gentleman that would give you the shirt off his back. He passed away in 2002.

"He was a musician. He was famous. He was one of the original Sons of the Pioneers. He wore red pointy boots, and he played guitar. He had a blondish-color wood Fender Stratocaster. He used to tell me, 'When you get older, this will be yours.' I was with him when he took that guitar to Thoroughbred Music in Tampa, Florida—we needed money bad. They gave him $200 for the guitar. We were standing on the sidewalk. We hadn't even walked away yet when some guy put my dad's guitar and a sign that read $4,500 on display in the front window.

"My drinking problem started because of going into bars when my dad would be playing with the band. I can't blame my father for my alcoholism. It was my choice to drink, not his. But I started out real young. I was only twelve years old. By fifteen I was an alcoholic, and I was drinking every day. But I got my GED, a little college, and my certificate of welding.

"The 2008 recession really hurt me. I broke my back, and it put me out of work. My wife separated from me due to life being so hard. I have a son; he's in Wisconsin. He had two step-siblings, and one night when I was locked up and he was three years old they found the kids on the streets at three in the morning. They put the kids in foster care. I fought to get my son back. But I haven't seen him since he was three; he's seventeen now. When he's eighteen and legal I'll try to find him. I'd really like to see what kind of person he is. My sister had him for a couple of years, and she told me he was like me. He was like his dad having trouble in school, she said. She had to let him go back to foster care. He went back with the family that had his sister and brother.

"I kept getting pulled over for traffic violations. When I was a teenager, I had DUIs. I quit drinking in 2000, that's when my life seemed to turn around, but then I was pulled over in 2004 for no license. I had no trouble from 2004 to 2009. Then in February 2009 there was a terrible ice storm. I was out of work, but I had a pickup truck and a chain saw, so I was cutting trees and hauling them off just to make some money, and then I was pulled over for expired plates. I didn't even know they were expired. It hinders me so much, not being able to get a license. The money's been the main issue. You have to pay the courts and attorneys and driver's license branches.

"When I get out of here, I'm getting away from my past. Starting fresh. My girlfriend, she's willing to move up here too. I'm looking for an apartment not too far from work. I'll do anything—ride a bicycle, take the bus, catch rides—anything to get it right.

"I've learned a lot since I've been here. I tell the counselors in substance abuse that part of my addiction is that I want it *now*. Even though I don't drink, I still have the addictive behavior. The trigger for drinking is what triggers the impatience."

This is where Father Dave comes into the picture.

"When Father Link first started the class was when I was aggravated all the time. But I listened to him. When he says something I take it to heart. Now I can catch myself getting angry. I never even realized some of the things I was doing! But Father Link has given me the tools. He says to sit back and listen to yourself. Pay attention to your body parts. Relax the parts that are uptight, any part that's hurting. He taught me about a mantra and how to come back to it in meditation. He is the main reason

I calmed down and can work for what I want. He told me, 'Don't give up. If you want something out of life, you have to work for what you want. You may not like someone's opinion, but listen to what they have to say and then use what is good from it.'

"He proves that one man can make a difference."

Re-entry programs strive to combine education with work internships. Not every man can get a job during the re-entry phase. Those who can are the lucky ones. Sean labored, earning twenty cents an hour, cleaning up forest detritus out at South Bend's Potato Creek State Park, which covers 3,480 acres, including the 327-acre Worster Lake.

"It was the middle of winter. Our job was to clean the fence line all the way around the park so that a new fence could be put in. I was hauling logs in wheelbarrows out through the snow a mile or more—it was so cold—and then loading the wood and branches onto a trailer. It was hard work, but I was glad to do it. It made the time go faster.

"We rode in a van to and from work. Jay, the guy who drives the van, is always complaining about his two little boys. But I tell him, 'You need to just go home and give them a hug. What are you going to do when they're fourteen or fifteen? You won't be able to give them a hug. Try a different approach when they don't want to get up in the morning. Tell them, Hey boys, if you get up and get dressed we can go to McDonald's.' "

Coming from someone who was not around to give his own son very many hugs, someone who had received precious few hugs himself, the advice Sean gave was poignant.

———————

In his Cage the Rage classes, Father Dave teaches that anger is a natural emotion, and the objective is to control that anger rather than never to be angry. He explains why anger past and present can exist simultaneously, and how to discern the difference between anger and aggression. He leads discussions about what causes anger and how prisoners can recognize the signs of impending anger by tuning in to their biofeedback systems. He coaches them on tuning in to when someone else is trying to push their buttons. Then he gives them the key to controlling a rising flood of anger. He tells them, "Ask yourself this question: *Is it worth it?*"

Bingo. Now they have a checkpoint. Here is where they can pause, ask that one simple question, and decide for themselves: Is my anger worth the consequences of my giving it full rein?

Garrick E. "Gary" Sparkman's life has taken him in and out of incarceration a couple of times. Gary grew up on the far south side of Chicago in a neighborhood known as the Wild 100s.

The Wild 100s is a stretch of neglected land that encompasses the streets from 100th to 138th. On May 27, 2010, ABC7 featured a special report on street violence. The segment began with an unqualified statement about violence: "Nowhere is it worse than in a neighborhood known as the Wild 100s."

Growing up, Gary was affiliated with a gang from a very young age. One of his friends was shot through the eye while Gary was standing right beside him. Gang turf fighting took the lives of several other friends, one of whom died in Gary's arms. But gang life was the only life he knew.

"I never had that teaching to be a father or a husband," Gary confides. "I had *one* friend who had a father."

Gary sold drugs but was known as "The Square" because he would not use them. This went on for years until Gary saw the light and decided that enough was enough. There was a violent standoff, and members of another gang brought in dogs that had been trained to attack. Gary was flat on the ground, and a rival gang member was pressing an Uzi into his stomach. Inside his mind, Gary prayed, "Lord, get me out of this. I'm tired. Please. Bless me to get me out of this gang. I don't want it no more."

Gary gives credit to the Lord for the miracle of his survival as well as for his having survived the "consequences" of opting out of gang affiliation.

He left gang activity behind, but he had not yet conquered his reactive temper. When he discovered that someone he loved was cheating on him, his violent reaction landed him at Indiana State Prison for ten years. It was in prison that Gary found his father figure, the man he came to know and love, sometimes referring to him as Father Link, sometimes as Doc. Because of his association with Father Dave, Gary was inspired to use his ten years to serve others.

"The Lord used me inside the prison walls at ISP. I spent my time in the lockup units sharing the Word. All of the gangs are in there. A lot of them knew me from Chicago. But the Lord opened my eyes to see the cry of the men in there. The majority questioned me. They asked, 'How did you do that? How did you get out with no consequences?' I told them, 'The Lord blessed me. I got out by the grace of God.' "

The final eighteen months of Gary's sentence were served at the South Bend Work Release Facility, where he was an avid student in Father Dave's courses on life skills and anger management.

"Talking with Father Link put the pieces of the puzzle right there where they need to go," he says. "His love. It stands out. How he cares. There's so much compassion in him. You see it from far away. He listens. When you sit down with him you know you have his full, undivided attention. A lot of the time that's what we need is someone to just listen. I saw that I could trust him, and so I shared the hurt that was in me. I poured it out to him. I was able to cry with him. He saw my hurt and my pain, and he shared some words of wisdom about it. He taught me about self-talk. How to think about the consequences of what am I gaining when I do this, and what do I have to lose.

"I like to just steal away and think. During those moments I could always see him, see the way he listens before he gives advice. In my quiet time I could hear his laugh."

Gary recalls that he also had to work very hard just to learn how to let go of the past and forgive himself for what he did wrong in his former life.

"We are our own worst critics. It's sometimes hard accepting the love of God and His forgiveness. It's hard to see His favor still on me, and to know that He's still there and I'm participating in His work. But Doc was that missing link to forgiving myself."

Not long after Gary's release, newly learned lessons were put to a dramatic test. It was a cold winter night. Gary was wearing his warmest coat, an old possession from his life before prison. It was a long coat made of fur and leather. Someone who knew him from the old days spotted him. He was well aware of Gary's temper. He also knew that Gary was out on probation. Hoping to provoke a violent reaction and get Gary in trouble, the man taunted, picked, and poked at Gary. Gary triumphed in two different ways. First, he kept his cool. Second, he sent a signal to the aggressor by calling the police.

In prison, smiles can be dangerous. Prisoners who smile can be ostracized, hurt, or even killed. A homophobic prisoner might interpret a smile as a sexual invitation; when this happens, woe to the one who smiled. Prisoners with entrenched, hard-core attitudes see smiles as a sign of weakness; the one who smiles is labeled "soft" and is excluded, snubbed, or targeted. The upshot of living in the prison subculture is a learned resistance to smiles or any other sign of friendliness. Those who are incarcerated for long sentences forget that smiling is even an option.

When it became clear that Gary was not going to engage, the assailant pulled out a knife and slashed the coat Gary was wearing. At this point, Gary initiated the self-talk he had practiced in Father Dave's classes. In his mind, he scoffed at the coat. He reminded himself that it was nothing but material stuff. Gary was able to see the man's violence as an attempt to control Gary's behavior and Gary's future. Instead of getting angry, Gary smiled. In fact, he laughed. When the man refused to stop, Gary called the police.

Prison society changes personalities. Father Dave sometimes uses the Keirsey Temperament Sorter-II, which is an easily administered personality test, so that prisoners can better understand their own personalities and those of other people. He tells them that research has shown a person's personality almost always stays the same throughout that person's lifetime, and that being placed in an abnormal society is the only situation in which a personality can change. Then he leads a discussion about how prisons are abnormal societies. Behind bars it's We vs. Them.

Prisoners and guards are forced to interact in abnormal patterns of behavior that are dominated by this warlike mentality.

Gary says, "As a result of this horrible environment, many men can't make an adjustment back into the outside. Anyone who is in for more than five or ten years has been institutionalized. It changes your mind. It makes you a different person. And without any spiritual and educational programs, there is nothing there to counterbalance all the negative."

But for the lessons he learned in Father Dave's classrooms, things would have ended differently for Gary on the night that somebody cut up his coat. "Everything that was taught to me by Doc and everything that God has invested in me kicked right in. I remember one real big guy in the fall semester stood up to testify at the end of one of our classes. He said, 'I used to think it took a man to punch someone out. But after what Doc has taught us, I know that it takes a real man to just walk away.' And I know that now, too. It takes a real man to just walk away."

Gary says that he has found his life's purpose. He wants to be a good father to his son and daughter. He also wants to help others avoid what he has gone through. He is a free man now. He is blessed with a steady job, which helps to stabilize his life at the same time as it allows him to dream. What he dreams of is coaching young people through the snares of inner-city poverty.

"Young people. If I could save them all, I would. I would do anything to keep them from ruining their lives. No one is telling them *It will happen to you.* They're being told about the glamour and about the money they can make, but they're little *peons!* Lord, these are BABIES! When you get them by themselves and talk to them, and they're feeling like life is all gone at fourteen, sixteen, eighteen years old and they're thinking of hanging themselves, you see the real kid in them. The baby in them. No one has taken the time to tell them about life. *It takes a village.* Where is that village today? If you're a good kid in a bad neighborhood, you're just considered weak, and you'll be taken advantage of. They will eat their lunch off of you. So you have to get tough, even if you want to be good.

"We need to give these kids some other opportunity. Their one opportunity now is in selling drugs. We need to give them another kind of job so they can earn money legally. We need to give them something worthwhile. Something worth living for."

Establishing equilibrium after being released from prison is every ex-offender's first challenge. Gary is one of the luckiest in that he has a job. He has been able to establish a living situation that allows him to be a reliable employee. But coming out of prison and starting over was tough. He did not own a bed or sheets, dishes, or cookware. Yet all the while that he was putting together a new life, Gary was dreaming of doing more.

"There is a reason and a purpose for everything," he says. "I know that now. I saw how God took someone like Father Link from being an attorney to being a priest. And I think, 'He is using Father Link to do something bigger than all of us.' I think that maybe Doc's calling is to challenge the judicial system about how they're running the prisons. I'm hopeful. It's been a long time coming. But everyone, *everyone*, has a calling."

As he struggled to establish a household and a new citizenship, Gary began to put some teeth into his dream of ministering to at-risk youth. He spread the word that he is available to speak to groups and individuals. He began to receive invitations to community events held in church basements and community rooms. Small though these speaking engagements may be, they are the highlights of his life.

A few thousand years ago another young man was just beginning his own public speaking career, a career that had been running, as they say, under the radar. The time had arrived for him to present his platform in no uncertain terms, so he climbed to the top of a knoll and prepared to deliver his first major public address.

Mesmerized by this man whose career was gathering steam, multitudes gathered. Though there were no cameras to capture the moment, one can almost see the shuffling and hear the murmuring as people settled in expectantly. No doubt, many sensed that they were about to witness a portentous event. Perhaps the elderly lowered themselves to sit on the gentle plains below the mount. Young parents must have juggled and hushed babes in arms, or shifted toddlers from hip to hip until at last everyone had quieted. The sea of faces tilted upward, and the gaze of thousands of eyes was trained on the slight figure standing atop the hill.

Using broad brushstrokes that highlight the contradictory nature of humanity, the speaker painted a new view of the purpose of life. His speech was peppered with curious juxtapositions. He said that those who are burdened by poverty, meekness, and sorrow are the most blessed of all. He talked about justice. He predicted that those who hunger and thirst for justice would be satisfied. He praised the merciful and the peacemakers, and he promised that they would themselves be rewarded with mercy and with peace. Henceforth, there would be no mistaking the fundamental tenets of his platform. In a fairly short sermon he showed how to recognize and follow a path that would lead to contentment and success.

This teaching of the Beatitudes set forth the mission of Jesus. It has inspired men and women great and small, historical and forgotten. It is Father Dave's favorite passage in Scripture.

The principal significance of Father Dave's life is that he follows his personal calling with faith and trust while at the same time permitting himself to be used as a bridge.

A link.

A healing force.

Father Dave's work can best be described as the construction of bridges by which those who are huddled at the suffering end of life are able to step across the divide. These bridges have been built with the brick and mortar of friendship and compassion. Having crossed over, Dave's camerados are able to strike out on better, truer, more purposeful life paths.

By remaining open to reinterpretations of his life's purpose, Dave has fulfilled his own personal destiny. "When I was dean, two law firms offered me a guaranteed million dollars a year, and they didn't understand why I turned the offers down. One senior partner said that he could come up with another $200,000 and throw in a BMW as well. But he missed the point. I wanted something more meaningful in my life. It was about *my* purpose in life.

"Barbara made me realize that I had the power to make a difference. I learned from her that I could do something about the poor. The homeless. The prisoners. She gave me a whole new perspective on how to teach law.

"I used to tell the students, 'Anybody can try a lawsuit. That's not hard work. What is hard work is settling a dispute.' I was hired by Winston, Strawn to be a business trial lawyer, and I had a lot of litigation. But I never once tried a case in court for the firm; I settled every case. And I did it in such a way that both sides felt that I had represented my client well since the objective was not to win.

"Chief Justice Burger told me, 'We have lawsuits and we have wars as a result of lawyers and politicians not understanding their jobs. Your clients are only entitled to justice.' And so for me the objective was always justice. My focus was 'What does justice require here? What ought to happen here?'

"I've worked with some of the best and some of the worst attorneys in the world. What I observed is that the best attorneys never thought about the law in assessing a case. They would look at a set of facts and determine from the facts what ought to happen. 'This is a hell of a good set of facts; my client ought to win.' Or, conversely, 'This is a terrible set of facts; my client ought to settle.' Then they would go back and prove it logically. When you find justice, then you can find the law that supports it. And so for me in my practice it was all about what ought to happen so that justice would be served, not what I could make happen by winning."

Going behind The Wall was a game-changer for Dave. His eyes were opened to the dire need to apply this same line of reasoning to the criminal justice system. With all of our nation's systems so broken, what *ought* to happen? Where and how will *justice* be served? How can all of us—the innocent public, the victims of crime, and the perpetrators of those crimes—win?

Cheering on his former dean in this daunting task is Father

Jim McDonald, who has left his position as counselor to President John I. Jenkins, CSC, to work among Holy Cross priests and brothers. Now serving as assistant provincial and steward with particular responsibility for Latin America, Father McDonald lives and works on the other side of "the Lake"—the "Lac" of the University of Notre Dame du Lac.

Framing the quintessential question, Father McDonald asks, "Will Dave be able to accomplish any kind of systemic change?" And he offers a sanguine assessment.

"He knows the details. But he also knows the big picture. He is consistent, committed, and persistent. He will follow through to the end. So I think that if the proposals that he comes up with become concrete, Dave will be able to persuade others. He's eloquent and persuasive. I mean, if you listen to him give a talk, he could sell you the Brooklyn Bridge and you'd love it in your backyard. He's just really, really effective."

In the late 1800s John Roebling dared to pursue the dream of connecting New York's two grand cities, Manhattan and Brooklyn. This bold, brilliant architect designed a truss system that was six times as strong as he thought it needed to be, and as a result the bridge remains long after other bridges built during that era have crumbled. More than a century after being constructed amidst iniquities that seemed certain to keep the structure from spanning the East River, Roebling's masterpiece stands as testimony of his vision, his determination, and his personal destiny.

Author David McCullough writes in *The Great Bridge*, his saga of how this epic feat was accomplished:

A bridge over the East River, joining the cities of New York and Brooklyn, had been talked about for nearly as long as anyone can remember. But nothing was done. The chief problem was always the East River, which is no river at all technically speaking, but a tidal strait and one of the most turbulent and in that day, especially, one of the busiest stretches of navigable salt water anywhere on earth. "If there is to be a bridge," wrote one man, "it must take one grand flying leap from shore to shore over the masts of the ships. There can be no piers or drawbridge. There must be only one great arch all the way across. Surely this must be a wonderful bridge."

Father Dave's Crime Peace Plan is the criminal justice system's Brooklyn Bridge. It takes grand, flying leaps between the shores of freedom and the shores of incarceration. Healing measures for every aspect of an ailing criminal justice system are included in this plan. Everyone in society will play some role in the resuscitation of systems that were placed on the thinnest of life-support measures decades ago. The plan details common-sense procedures to bridge the divides between judges, prosecutors, defense counsel, prison administrators, victims of crime, prisoners, and citizens.

All that remains is for Father Dave to tell America about his Crime Peace Plan. Optimist that he is, he is already imagining just how great it will look in our backyards.

For you are but a bridge, a passage, and your life's reality lies in that which you transform.

—Antoine de Saint-Exupéry, *Wisdom of the Sands*

Coda

On Saturday mornings after having celebrated Mass at Little Flower Catholic Church, Father Dave stops at his usual place and chooses a bouquet of flowers to take to Barbara. After paying for them, he eases himself into his car by folding his bum knee through the door.

It's only a couple of miles to campus from Little Flower. Turning right from Angela Boulevard onto Notre Dame Avenue, he anticipates the golden dome and smiles when he sees it glowing in the sunlight. To the left is the cemetery that was established in 1843 by Notre Dame founding president Edward R. Sorin, CSC. Father Dave steers his car through the wrought-iron gates of Cedar Grove Cemetery's entrance.

He makes a striking figure, dressed in black shirt, black slacks, and black double-breasted jacket, the white clerical collar at his throat. He clutches Barbara's bouquet in both hands, with his arms extended in front of him. It is an image that calls to mind a suitor in Sunday best coming to call on his ladylove. He crosses the lawn with long strides, stopping at an oblong granite chunk that rises ten inches from the ground.

He bends and places white daisies, the flowers his late wife loved most, into the vase affixed to the headstone. Then with his right hand he enacts a little ritual. He brings his fingertips to his lips and presses a kiss upon them. He touches those fingers to the headstone, giving a kiss to the woman who owns his heart. His hand flutters back to his mouth and he places another kiss upon his fingertips. This kiss is delivered to Little Barbara. After Barbara's death, Dave arranged for his daughter's small casket to be brought to Cedar Grove, where it now rests beside that of Little Barbara's mother. His hand does the dance one more time and Barbara gets a second kiss.

Dave straightens and crosses just a few steps away to a sleek granite bench nestled against the wrought-iron fence that separates cemetery from campus. Chiseled into the granite is LINK, and just below is the official seal of the University of Notre Dame. Taking a seat, Dave gazes at the headstone and lets his thoughts wander.

Barbara.

God only knows where I'd be without you.

Dave watches a montage of his life in his mind's eye. There was Barbara, of course, and their amazing children and beautiful grandchildren. There were the six careers on six continents. There were his clients and his partners. His students—those wonderful students—and that incredible faculty. His loyal friends. His terrific family. His heroes. His mentors. Father Ted. He sees the disenfranchised, the poor, the homeless, and the prisoners. Looking at the long arch of his life helps him put it all into perspective.

He is in his midseventies. If he has any chance of getting this done in whatever time remains to him on this earth, he may have to make some hard choices. He loves bringing the messages of friendship and redemption to his brothers, but from deep within his heart comes a reluctant admission that some of the time that he has been spending with the prisoners must be sacrificed. It may be the only way that he will be able to articulate and promote his comprehensive plan for healing a criminal justice system that is bloodied and broken. He has so many ideas that could be implemented right now, ideas that would save lives as well as money.

He has been mistaken in thinking that this is the sage period of his life. There is still much too much work to be done.

He'd best get to it.

It is a golden moment that must be shared with the one who helped bring him to this point. His throat constricts. His eyes glisten in the sunlight.

"Barbara," he whispers, "thank you."

The people who are crazy enough to think they can change the world are the ones who do. — Steve Jobs

Afterword

A CRIME PEACE PLAN
by David T. Link

My Crime Peace Plan outlines suggestions for correcting what have become fatal flaws in our criminal justice system. It has been designed so that traditional concepts of justice are applied to the criminal justice system. Its objective is to achieve true justice for victims and victims' families, for those who are accused and convicted, and for society at large.

For several decades, America has been waging a so-called War on Crime. Nonetheless, many aspects of the crime cycle have been in fast-forward. As a result, in 2013 we are sitting atop a sociological volcano, and there are rumblings below. We are in danger of escalating this "war" to an alarming degree, and unfortunately, we have no exit strategy. The collateral damage is the growing number of victims and victims' families. Some additional serious consequences of the lost battles in this war include overcrowded courts, overworked defense counsel, overzealous prosecutors, misleading plea bargains, unreasonably high rates of incarceration, overcrowded correctional facilities, and sky-rocketing corrections budgets.

In 2010, in the state of Indiana alone, where I am privileged to serve as a volunteer chaplain, there were 27,132 residents living in corrections facilities. The cost to the state was $1,767,378 per day. Volumes have been written on the alarming situation that exists all across the nation. The crisis is so generalized, it is tempting to allow the sheer profundity of the problems to paralyze even a modest attempt at reform. And yet a start must be made somewhere.

At the core of the problem is thinking of the crime cycle in military terms. Strategies for "winning" are parallel to desperate tactics used in military campaigns. We have tried tactical maneuvers such as lock 'em up and throw away the key, longer sentences, adding new crimes to the list of felonies requiring incarceration, and, following the old pirate philosophy of "the beatings will continue until morale improves," intensifying the punishment. These strategies have, in fact, produced no solutions. They have provided minimal deterrence while exacerbating the crime cycle. Significantly, these ineffective strategies have violated many constitutional rights, wasted countless lives, and incited exaggerated negative public opinion about the prisoners of this curious war. Most important, by not treating the sickness of crime, we have jeopardized the safety and security of law-abiding citizens.

The number of citizens that America incarcerates is, like her prisons, disproportionately outsized in comparison with global statistics. We comprise 5 percent of the world's population but fully 25 percent of the world's incarcerated population. In 2008 the United States incarcerated 2.3 million people, more than the top thirty-five European countries *combined*. Proposals to expand the War on Crime by building more prisons constitute a flawed formula that is destined to compound our many failures.

Furthermore, incarceration has become prohibitively expensive. Incarceration budgets are costing taxpayers in excess of $75 billion annually. Though the dollars shift from year to year, the overall trend remains: it is well recognized that it is less expensive and more effective to invest in programs that treat people outside of prison than it is to lock these same people up inside prison.

In considering the high cost of incarceration, we also need to think about the financial and social costs of wrongful convictions. In the state of Illinois, for example, a "seven-month investigation by the Better Government Association (BGA) and the Center on Wrongful Convictions (CWC) reveals that the wrongful convictions of 85 men and women for violent crimes in Illinois have cost taxpayers $214 million, and imprisoned innocent people for more than 900 years. Meanwhile the real perpetrators committed nearly 100 felonies."

My Crime Peace Plan is not about how to be more lenient or more sympathetic to criminals, nor is it only about saving money in federal and state corrections' budgets. The Crime Peace Plan is a populist project. It is a people's plan. It is about keeping our streets, neighborhoods, and homes safe and secure. Most people are under the illusion that locking up criminals for long periods of time creates safer environments, but the opposite is true.

While the cycle of crime has numerous forms, each is vicious and has a centrifugal force. Often, the cycle begins because a dysfunctional family, a bad neighborhood, an addiction, or a rebellion against societal pressure leads an individual into serious criminal activity. If such a person is incarcerated without any attempt to treat underlying causes, the cycle spins out of control. The incarcerated person is exposed to higher education of a destructive sort. Schooled in the art of lying and manipulating, he or she becomes, as a result, a more sophisticated, expert social deviant, and the expansion of the crime cycle continues.

With the criminal separated from his or her loved ones, the family bottoms out. Spouse and children are forced to deal with life with even fewer resources than they had before. Crime, which is one of the most infectious diseases in all of society, spreads even further when prisoners re-enter society without there having been any attempt to treat the causative, underlying problems that sent them to prison in the first place.

I, for one, do not want a bitter, criminally coached manipulator, or any of his or her family, living anywhere close to me. The answer to this conundrum lies in treatment before re-entry. It is imperative that help is made available to those inmates who seek help.

Every law-abiding citizen should demand drastic changes in the criminal justice system, changes that will interrupt the crime cycle. Certain causes of crime such as poverty and inadequate housing will take many, many years to address. But breaking the crime cycle by treating the sicknesses behind criminal behavior can begin immediately.

The Crime Peace Plan outlines dramatic changes that can be made in America's criminal justice system. If the proposed reforms seem too drastic, we will do well to remember that the problems are so great and have developed over such a long period of time that an extraordinary reversal is in order.

Before outlining the Crime Peace Plan, it is necessary to clear our minds of some old myths. First, some profound confusion about the word "justice" has developed. Many people believe that justice is synonymous with revenge, as in "I will never have justice until the perpetrator of this terrible crime gets the same as the victim" or "I can never forgive that horrible person; I want justice." The sad truth is that vengeance will never restore matters to the former condition. The execution of a murderer, for example, cannot bring the person who was murdered back to life. It does not matter how minor or heinous the crime, no consequence visited upon another person will remedy the crime itself. Revenge is not the answer. Revenge is the culmination of bitterness and rage, and bitterness hurts the one in whom it is harbored far more than it hurts the object of that spite. Former President of South Africa Nelson Mandela has observed, "Resentment is like drinking poison and then hoping it will kill your enemies."

Some people think that the word "justice" means treating everyone equally. This is also a misinterpretation. Philosophers grappling with the concept of justice have pointed to its aspect of specialization. For Plato, justice exists on two planes: the personal, where justice is to the soul what good health is to the physical body; and the social, where justice means not the superior strength of those in control but the harmoniousness of the whole. Plato's student, Aristotle, argued a theory of natural law. Here, laws that societies choose to enact must be consistent with laws of nature, and unjust laws are those that contradict natural law. Thus the system constructed by a society to promote and serve justice is, in effect, a construct for a moral compass that will inform that culture. The Crime Peace Plan is designed to apply traditional concepts of justice to the criminal justice system, with the objective of achieving true justice for victims and victims' families, those who are accused and convicted, state budgets, and society at large.

My years working in prisons have shown me that the secret to success in prison administration lies in the attitude about the purpose of incarceration. Prisons can and should serve a role in protecting the public by separating people who are dangerous from citizens. That being said, the reasons that prisons exist turn on three primary objectives: public safety, security, and removal from society. When the purposes of incarceration are limited to just these three, it follows that everyone in the system will be treated identically. This type of narrow thinking ensures that what goes on in our prisons is systematic depersonalization. In a word, offenders are warehoused.

In thinking about implementing a healing plan as a strategy for breaking the crime cycle, it is helpful to conceptualize jails and prisons as functioning like hospitals. Prisons should be viewed as centers where the convicted are given necessary and appropriate treatment before they are returned to society.

This Crime Peace Plan resolves problems that presently are clogging the criminal justice system. The Plan is *not* about how to be lenient or more sympathetic to criminals. The real beauty of this plan is that everyone—legal practitioners, professionals working in the incarceration industry, and citizens—can participate in making it a reality.

OBJECTIVES OF THE CRIME PEACE PLAN

1. Change the mission of the system from punishment to healing
2. Change the system from adversarial to collaborative
3. Appoint rather than elect prosecutors
4. Oblige all lawyers to engage in or to support criminal defense as a condition of practice
5. Establish a special code of ethics for prosecution and criminal defense
6. Establish an accurate and uniform definition of crime
7. Establish indeterminant and consistent standards of sentencing
8. Convert jails and prisons to places that are concerned with the diagnosis of and treatment for the social illnesses that have brought each person to incarceration
9. Have sentence modification determinations made by

people who know the present status of the incarcerated
and the readiness of the receiving community
10. Provide tax incentives for employers who hire recovering
ex-prisoners

1. Healing versus Punishment

An essential premise of this Crime Peace Plan is the substitution
of a healing attitude in place of a motivation to punish. Anthro-
pologists theorize that as the hunters and gatherers of the world
moved into villages they discovered a need for experts who would
perform activities that were beyond the scope of individual solutions. The expert whose concern was healing the body became
the professional who treated sickness with the intent of extending life and improving physical well-being. Whether referred to as
a witch doctor, herb healer, or any other title, this specialist was
the ancestor of those presently engaged in our medical professions. Another expert dealt with healing the spirit, or the soul.
Through prayers and incantations, this faith healer or shaman
was the precursor of today's clergy.

It has been largely forgotten that there was a third type of
healer in ancient civilizations. This expert specialized in problems
of living in community—problems such as property ownership,
the transfer of wealth or property, or what to do about people
who violated societal norms. The important point here is that
these ancestors of today's judges and legal practitioners were engaged in healing; they had little or no interest in punishment or
in separating people from society.

Judges and lawyers would do well to remember their origins.
Chief Justice Warren Burger said, "Lawsuits, like wars, often
occur when lawyers and statesmen fail in their role as healers

and peacemakers. This healing function ought to be the primary role of the lawyer in the highest conception of our profession."

2. Collaboration

Criminal justice is not a game. Any loss becomes a loss for society. Our homes, streets, and neighborhoods are safe when the life of a criminal turns toward proactive citizenship. This requires that all elements of the system—police, prosecutors, defense counsel, judges, incarceration facilities, and community corrections—work together to help those who commit crimes and to help the children who have been immersed in particularly destructive environments.

Consider a man accused of multiple driving offenses. In a system committed to a punishment goal, every government participant joins the discipline frenzy, resulting in excessive and unnecessary sentences. The accompanying separation from family often adds detrimental consequences for future generations.

In contrast, when police, prosecutors, defense counsel, and incarceration facilities collaborate on a healing agenda, everyone is more likely to arrive at a community corrections solution that is better suited to help both the community and the offender even as the solution interrupts crime cycles in future generations.

3. Prosecutors

The Crime Peace Plan proposes that *all prosecutors be appointed rather than elected.*

Prosecutors are public servants. As such they must be free and unencumbered so that they can represent all aspects of society. It is not uncommon to hear prosecutors proclaiming that their professional purpose is to be tough on crime. But history does not support such a statement. The ideal is that prosecutors are elected to shine the light of truth on all aspects of criminal prosecutions.

The pressure of running for election or re-election forces many prosecutors to campaign based on so-called successful prosecutions, including plea bargains. As a result, prosecutors are often motivated to be more concerned about winning cases than about discovering the truth. Prosecutors who remain unencumbered by campaign motives are in the best position to initiate these desperately needed treatment processes for offenders who need help, not punishment. Thus, in healing terms, the prosecutor is akin to an emergency room diagnostician.

The Crime Peace Plan provides that prosecutorial appointments will be made by the local judiciary. The judiciary is in a premier position to oversee that the objectives of protecting and healing are being met by the prosecutors. Therefore, the judiciary should evaluate and monitor the prosecutorial performance in serving the highest ideals of justice. The public plays a role in the process by critiquing the local judiciary and responding via their electoral power in passing judgment on the quality of prosecutor appointments.

Plea bargains can be a helpful tool for prosecutors. But plea bargains can also be abused. For instance, prosecutors can use the threat of felonies carrying long prison terms to extract pleas of guilt to lesser charges. While this practice of overcharging in order to get a plea bargain agreement is often used as a strategy for clearing cases without having to take them to trial, it also becomes valuable to prosecutors who are running for re-election.

It seems obvious to state that plea bargains must never be used for the purpose of saving time and/or money, and that they should never be agreed to as a result of threats made to the accused. Plea bargains must remain in their purest form as a strategy for balancing the needs of the community, including victims and victims' families, with the best healing interests of the accused. In other words, plea bargains should be a *bargain* for *all* of the stakeholders. *Upon agreement, plea bargains should be considered as contracts rather than offers.*

Prosecutors will have one shot at approaching the bench with a plea bargain. If a plea bargain is rejected by the court, the prosecutor must then focus on trying the case.

The above restructuring of the prosecutorial role demands that prosecutors be especially well qualified public servants. An important feature of this Crime Peace Plan is its insistence on special continuing education for all prosecutors. As the needs of the community change, as research suggests new methods for reversing criminal behavior, and as more sophisticated and effective treatment methodologies become available, it is essential that prosecutors become cutting-edge experts in healing and the law.

4. Defense Counsel

People who are accused of criminal activity and who are unable to pay for counsel enter the system having two choices: representation pro se (self-representation) or representation by public defenders. While there are many highly competent public defenders, most are overworked and underpaid. Furthermore, idealistic lawyers who are called to the criminal justice specialty by noble intentions often suffer from high burnout. Public defenders and appointed counsel endure enormous pressure to turn over cases as quickly as possible due to meager or nonexistent compensation.

There is no doubt that there exists in America a great divide in the quality of defense given to poor clients as compared with the kind of representation given to clients who have financial resources. There are too few attorneys who can defend indigents with the thoroughness and passion that is required of good representation. To solve this problem that begets more problems, the Crime Peace Plan proposes that *every attorney is required to provide legal representation (counseling, trial, appeal, or sentence modification) for at least one criminal defendant at all times during his or her practice. Those attorneys who are unqualified to serve as effective criminal defense counsel can opt instead to subsidize the legal representation of at least one criminal defendant at all times.* Lawyers may buy out of this standing obligation only by paying into a special defense fund an amount of money equal to the average cost of criminal defense. This special defense fund will act as a reservoir of funds reserved to better compensate public defenders and appointed counsel.

5. Codes of Ethics

Legal professions already have detailed rules of professional responsibility. This Crime Peace Plan calls for expanding these rules to detail ethical duties of prosecutors and criminal defense counsel.

Truly successful prosecution that seeks to uncover the truth is hard work. It involves responsibilities and skills that differ from those used by police, judges, and other trial lawyers. As provided for in this Crime Peace Plan, a distinct prosecutor's code of ethics will emphasize:

- the prosecutor's duty to represent the widest spectrum of citizens rather than just the victim, the victim's family, and the police
- the prosecutor's professional responsibility to seek the truth, including a duty to correct defense counsel's errors

as well as the duty to probe, examine, and question police
reports rather than reflexively defend them
* the prosecutor's ethical responsibility to divulge all
evidence to the court, even if that evidence is unfavorable
to the prosecution

This prosecutor's code of ethics defines the prosecutor in
traditional terms as an arm of the court that is dedicated to
bringing forth the truth while brokering a healing for society and
for the accused.

The code of ethics will specify that the obligation of robust
criminal defense, advice regarding the best treatment for the
healing of the pertinent criminal behavior, and buying out are
mandatory assessments on every practicing lawyer. In representing an accused or a convicted person, it is essential that the attorney be the primary source of information for the accused.
Under no circumstances should a client be "talked into" a plea
bargain.

Law work is a continuum: the attorney who takes on a trial
or a plea bargain should be prepared to also handle appeals or
other postconviction remedies.

6. Definitions and Categories of Crimes

Many states have delineated only two distinct categories of
crime: violent and nonviolent (or property). Categorization this
simplistic is counterproductive and contributes greatly to the depersonalization of crimes and criminals. Throwing all crimes and
all prisoners into such broad categories would be like medical
practitioners dividing all patients into just two categories.

Many violent criminals turn their lives around. On the other
hand, the prison experience can inspire people convicted of

property crimes to become violent. It is clear that supplemental classifications such as minor, moderate, drug-induced, fraud, pedophilia, and adult sex-related should be added to the two overarching categorizations, violent and property. Categorization that is more descriptive and specific will be helpful to prosecutors, defense counsel, the judiciary, and those employed in corrections work when screening prisoners who are eligible for sentence modification or early release.

Our challenge is to define crime and achieve uniformity. According to staff writers at Criminal Justice USA, "some actions that would cause the typical American to go to prison for a significant period of time aren't even considered crimes in other countries around the world." Within the United States, although the majority of incarcerated persons are in prison due to the use, possession, or selling of drugs, or because of committing crimes while under the influence of alcohol or other drugs, there is a wide variety of laws regarding the felonious sale and possession of drugs.

To alleviate one aspect of this dilemma, the Crime Peace Plan proposes that recreational drugs (that is, not physical gateway drugs) be regulated. The regulation of drugs is not to be confused with the decriminalization of drugs. The regulation of drugs would entail recreational drugs being sold in state stores or under state supervision, exactly as is now the case for alcohol and tobacco.

If we remove the use and possession of recreational drugs from the cycle of crime/profit/punishment/recidivism, the monies now funneling into organized crime and gangs will be radically undercut. We will also be able to establish meaningful control of the abuse of recreational drugs.

Typically, the drug crime cycle works as follows. It begins when recreational drugs are either given or sold at a deep discount to a susceptible person with the express intent of making

the drug attractive to a vulnerable target. Once a person becomes dependent (the street term is "hooked"), the purchase
price for the drug is increased. Often the user turns to crime to
support the new addiction ("habit"). Researchers have determined that certain recreational drugs (for example, alcohol and
marijuana) are not physical gateway drugs—that is, they do not
physically cause escalation to the use of hard narcotics. They are
social gateway drugs in that they introduce recreational users to
other persons involved in hard narcotics. This constitutes a very
compelling reason that we must get recreational drugs off the
street and away from gangs and professionals who benefit finan-
cially each time someone is initiated into the drug culture.

There are many advantages to this proposed system. Recreational drugs will be sold at prices that will steal the thunder from
black market sales. This will reduce the number of people who
turn to a life of crime in order to support a habit; users will no
longer be at the mercy of unscrupulous suppliers who raise prices
at will. A significant number of crimes will be taken off the street.

State sales of recreational drugs will entail meaningful state
regulations, including:

- personal identification and registration
- restrictions on the amount that can be sold to each
  individual
- limitations on the number of sales that can be made to
  any one person in a specified period
- strict reporting requirements

Crimes unaffected by this Crime Peace Plan are DUI, or driving under the influence; private dealing or trafficking in any kind
of drugs; selling to minors; and selling in geographic areas in
which minors are vulnerable targets.

The Crime Peace Plan supports the enrollment in effective, meaningful treatment programs of those who are possessing and using hard narcotics.

7. The Judicial System and Sentencing

The heart of a healthy, fully functioning criminal justice system is the judiciary. In a system designed to heal rather than punish, the criminal courts are to the legal profession what the clinic is to the medical profession: it is the privilege and duty of the courts to diagnose and prescribe remedy. When a criminal case reveals the truth, the court is positioned to diagnose the problem and prescribe treatment for the convicted offender. Unfortunately, at the present time, the courts are saddled with restrictive sentencing systems, overcrowded dockets, and the public misconception that revenge is a synonym for justice.

In those jurisdictions where it exists, determinative sentencing places unreasonable limitations on the discretion of trial courts. A determinative sentence is one in which a convicted criminal is given a sentence with a finite term of X number of years. With a determinative sentencing scheme, the judge usually is limited to three basic alternatives:

- so as to cover all possibilities, treat the convicted person harshly by imposing the maximum sentence available
- sentence all persons convicted of the same crime (under the same conditions) to the same incarceration period, even if one individual has a much better chance than another of changing his or her behavior
- dismiss the case when the judge feels that the minimum determinative sentence is unjust

Often it is understood that there is a possibility of reducing the amount of time served with good behavior. Determinative sentencing, arising out of the conflagration of the War on Drugs, has not fulfilled the mission with which it was charged. Certainty of punishment is not linked to the deterrence of crime. Moreover, determinative sentencing poisons the criminal justice system as a result of restricting decisions down the line.

A simple example will illustrate. Two persons are convicted of the same crime under similar conditions. Both are given forty-year sentences, and the understanding is that each will do twenty years, in a two-for-one "good time" system. One of the prisoners does everything to turn his or her life around, while the other inmate does nothing. Absent a sentence modification, both prisoners will be released after having served the same amount of time in prison. This even though one demonstrated an early readiness to return to society, while society is most definitely safer if the other remains incarcerated for the full term. (Please note also that the matured, reformed offender is unnecessarily incurring public expense while he or she is occupying prison space.)

In contrast, under a *flexible, or indeterminant, sentencing* system (one in which a range of years is handed down as a sentence), if someone is sentenced for a term of ten to eighty years, it is possible to release the deserving person who has turned his or her life around after the tenth year. The person who has done nothing to change his or her life pattern can be kept in prison for the full term of eighty years. A flexible sentencing program, that is, one that specifies minimum to maximum, has the added benefit of allowing flexibility to key professionals who will be making decisions—corrections facility administrators, Re-entry Courts, probation and parole administrators, and so on. Certainly flexible sentencing, with good time as a consideration for release, makes sense in any program dedicated to treat the sicknesses behind criminal behavior.

One of the major problems in sentencing, of course, is inconsistency from jurisdiction to jurisdiction. A person may get up to four times the incarceration sentence in one county that he or she would have received in an adjacent county.

The first step of the best answer to this situation is to establish uniform state standards for minimum and maximum sentences designated for particular crimes. It would be most helpful to the system if a national organization of experts such as the American Law Institute would publish recommendations of uniform state standards.

The second step to gaining consistency in sentencing standards is critical: if a trial judge or a jury deviates from the state standard in either mitigation or aggravation, under the provisions of this Crime Peace Plan the trial judge shall be required to render a written explanation for the deviation. The written explanation of deviation from state standards will:

- list all factors taken into account by the trial judge
- contain an explanation of the trial judge's opinion about proper treatment of the convicted person
- be periodically transmitted to the state court of appeals or the state supreme court as appropriate to a particular state

This requirement ought not be considered as a limitation on the discretion of the trial judge but as an incentive for that trial judge to provide an individualized healing solution for the convicted person, even as accountability to victims, victims' families, and the general public is maintained.

8. Incarceration

The Crime Peace Plan, while it neither is critical of present correctional facility administration nor advocates leniency for those convicted of crime, targets policies that undercut the stated prison mission of rehabilitation. The resources needed to attempt rehabilitation simply have not been allocated to prison administrators. Thus administrators are faced with a conundrum. Even if they want to provide rehabilitation for their prisoners, they are unable to do so.

It is a mistake to assume that the prison population is made up of a homogeneous group in which everyone can be treated the same. Each prisoner enters the correctional system with distinct problems and needs and would benefit from an individual plan. No matter the number of incarcerated people who do not turn their lives around, there will always be a significant percentage that can, and will, respond to intervention.

It may be helpful to view the business of incarceration with the perspective offered by Mark Levenhagen, superintendent of Westville Correctional Facility in Indiana. Superintendent Levenhagen describes his professional responsibility using an analogy to NASCAR (National Association for Stock Car Racing).

"Many people think we are like garage attendants—that we take cars damaged in competition and lock them into a garage. This is an inaccurate view. More accurately, we are like the pit crew. It is our job to get damaged cars back into the race."

Westville's assistant superintendent, Andrew Pazera, states, "It is not our job to punish these offenders. Coming to prison, being unable to go home at night, and being away from their families—that IS their punishment."

At Louisiana State Prison (known more familiarly as Angola), the largest prison in the country, Warden N. Burl Cain has proven that moral rehabilitation is key to public safety and prison stability. More than five thousand human beings are housed at Angola. Most understand that they will never be released from behind bars. And yet this is not a violent place. Cain's secret? A spiritual atmosphere is fostered. Why? Cain has seen that the hope of eternal life gives purpose and meaning to the lives of inmates. Warden Cain and his staff have transformed one of the nation's most violent prisons into a quintessential model for prison reform.

Warehousing creates a backlash of violence. In a system where human beings are warehoused, everyone—offenders who are trying to change their thinking and their behaviors as well as those who are *not* trying to change—becomes more frustrated than they were when they arrived at the facility. Those who maintain exemplary behavior have reason to believe that the world is against them, and that it is pointless to continue to mature socially. But when administrative decision-making similar to that utilized by Warden Cain is employed, the prison atmosphere becomes one of healing. Discovering that there is a purpose to life is a watershed experience that causes better behaviors to spring from better-thinking individuals.

Whatever the number of inmates who are able to find their better selves, be it great or small, society is advantaged. Individuals whose lives are being wasted will return to society better equipped and highly motivated to make positive contributions.

For a prison to have a healing environment, there must be three major components in operation: minimal idle time, education, and inspiration.

Idle time is indeed the devil's workshop. An individual who languishes in his or her cell has little to do but think of ways to get into trouble. *Everyone* who is not confined to some sort of special segregation unit should have a work responsibility. This is not just a matter of the state receiving benefits to compensate for shelter and food. This is a powerful way for the inmates' time to be occupied and for their energies to be refocused.

Educational programs are essential. Most inmates who will re-enter society need skills education in order to be employable upon release. It makes sense to help these people acquire skills during, rather than after, incarceration, as an uneducated ex-felon is almost surely to become a recidivist. Therefore the number of education programs in jails and prisons, including skills training, must be maximized.

Anger management training and substance abuse programs ought to be mandatory. These courses should be presented in a timely way—that is, at the beginning, not the end, of prison stays.

Assistant Superintendent Pazera reminds us, "Everyone, including inmates, is searching for the missing piece in the puzzle of his or her life." A person must first have awareness of life's purpose in order to restart a stalled life. Such inspiration often comes from religious or spiritual beliefs. Inspiration is often the key that unlocks hearts and minds that have never understood that they have been born into this world for a reason. Without moral inspiration during incarceration, increased recidivism, a continuation of the crime cycle, and an increase in criminal violence are inevitable.

Many correctional institutions are purely reactive. These facilities appropriately punish bad behavior. Unfortunately, they also inappropriately punish. What the reactive system does that is so wrong is to punish innocent, well-behaving prisoners right along with the one or two who have behaved in such a way that they have earned a negative consequence. This technique does not accomplish desired objectives. Not only does it not work; it often creates a destructive backlash. As one inmate put it, "If I'm going to get punished for something I didn't do, I may as well do the things that will lead to punishment!"

Reaction-only systems are unbalanced. They are therefore

ineffective. What is missing from purely reactive systems is positive reinforcement. A proactive system of rewards must be established in our prisons to balance out the present system of reactive punishment.

Many rewards for good behavior are available to prison administrators. These include special privileges, permission to participate in special programs, and reduction of incarceration time (known as "good time").

The ultimate reward for any prisoner is getting out of prison. In the spirit of hope, a prisoner can be greatly motivated by the possibility of working his or her way out of prison life. When a facility acts as a hospital for healing, it rewards a person for turning his or her life around in this way. Nothing produces progress as much as being rewarded for progress. In each facility, the well-behaved prisoner should be moved to a more desirable unit within the facility based on his or her good behavior. Similarly, a prisoner should be moved to a different facility based on consistently better behavior and availability of education programs.

9. Sentence Modification

What happens if an incarcerated person turns his or her life around? Under what conditions can a person be returned to society? We are not concerned here with when mistakes of law have been made at the trial level. Our appellate court system is designed to catch and correct those errors. What we are concerned with here is what happens to someone who turns his or her life around during incarceration. Do we permit such a person to continue to languish in prison? Do we allow that life to be wasted?

The major question in any system for early release is: how do we decide which inmates are ready? The answer lies in making an evaluation based on the *current status* of an inmate. What I mean here is that the inmate's readiness is judged not on the crime or the sentence (that is, the past) but on the present (the mental and emotional state of being) and the future (what strategies are in place that will help ensure the inmate's successful transition to the outside).

Often those who are making decisions about parole, commutation, or sentence modification are totally unfamiliar with the person and/or with his or her current behavior patterns. Decisions about early release are therefore based on the nature of the original crime rather than on whether the candidate is now on the right path and can become a productive member of society.

A plan to personalize sentence modification can be structured at each prison facility. The key participants in this healing process are:

- the prison facility's superintendent/warden
- the prison facility's Sentence Modification Board
- the local community's Re-entry Court

A model procedure for identifying candidates for early release is as follows:

1. Any staff member of a prison facility may nominate an eligible incarcerated person for sentence modification.
2. No staff member may nominate more than one incarcerated person for sentence modification during a calendar month.
3. To be eligible for nomination, an incarcerated person must have served either ten years or one-half of the minimum sentence, whichever is less.
4. To be eligible for nomination, an incarcerated person must be free of a Class A violation for at least one year

and free of a Class B violation for at least six months prior to nomination.

5. All nominations for sentence modification shall go before a facility Sentence Modification Board, whose members have been named by the facility superintendent. This Modification Board shall be composed of no less than three members, including, where possible, a representative of the custody staff and a chaplain or other spiritual advisor who is employed by the Department of Correction.

6. At no time shall any offender be informed of the name of any nominator or the name of any staff member(s) appointed to the Sentence Modification Board.

7. The Modification Board shall meet at least once each month to consider nominations.

8. If the Sentence Modification Board is unanimous in its decision to recommend a prisoner for early release, the nomination shall proceed to the superintendent, who may agree with the board's recommendation. The superintendent may also send the matter back to the Sentence Modification Board for a rehearing, asking that the board reconsider in light of the superintendent's written comments.

9. Sentence modification includes, but is not limited to, sentence reduction, parole or probation, work release, community correction, house arrest, release, or other appropriate action, with whatever restrictions and conditions are deemed advisable.

10. The entire process for sentence modification shall be confidential until such time as a nomination is before the Re-entry Court.

11. If the Modification Board's final decision on the

nomination is in favor of modification, its recommendation shall be sent to a Re-entry Court.

12. Under no circumstances shall a prosecutor or judge from
the original criminal trial be appointed to serve on the
Re-entry Court.

13. Members of the Re-entry Court shall be familiar with the
geographic area where the incarcerated person is to reside
after modification and with the resources available to this
person. Members of the Re-entry Court shall understand
that their responsibility is to establish and develop a
system for reducing the prison population in the state
while protecting the safety and security of the citizens.

14. Re-entry Courts shall be given all files applicable to a
nominee's case. Whenever feasible, the Re-entry Court
shall seek psychiatric analysis of the nominee's behavior.

15. Decisions of the Re-entry Court on matters of early release
are appealable by either the state or by the incarcerated
person.

The above sample plan for sentence modification is particular to the Indiana criminal justice system and to similar
programs. It should, however, make it clear that whatever the
jurisdiction, all re-entry recommendations must be placed in
the hands of people who know the facts about current inmate
behavior. Furthermore, there must be participation in decisions
about sentence modifications by a local court that has an inti-
mate knowledge of the community into which the prisoner will
be released.

10. Post Re-entry

If a person who has been released from a jail or prison is to avoid
recidivism, that person ordinarily needs the following support:

- a reason to change, that is, a purpose to life
- a decent, safe place to live
- a job that pays a living wage
- transportation between the residence and the job site
- sobriety
- a support group (for example, a church, temple, or nonprofit organization)

By far the hardest need to fill is employment. Today's economy makes it difficult for anyone, let alone a former felon, to find employment. The Crime Peace Plan therefore proposes a hiring incentive in the form of tax credits for prospective employers of ex-prisoners, war-zone military veterans, and homeless persons.

This would require federal legislation along the following lines:

1. An employer of a Worker Credit Eligible Employee shall receive a federal tax credit equal to the employee's base compensation on the following schedule:

YEARS OF EMPLOYMENT	CREDIT
1	100 percent
2	80 percent
3	60 percent
4	40 percent
5	20 percent

2. A Worker Credit Eligible Employee is any person who has been unemployed for at least the previous twelve months, or has been discharged from war zone military service within the past six months, or has been released from incarceration within the last six months.

3. Base compensation as used herein is an amount equal to the employee's wages or salary, not including benefits or bonuses.
4. The tax credit schedule will also apply to self-employed ex-felons, veterans, and homeless persons.

It will be necessary for government economists to compute the net cost of this legislation. But considering both welfare and social costs, such a system is likely to be economically beneficial for the government as well as a stimulus to the economy.

The War on Crime, like most wars, is not only shockingly expensive but it leaves lasting scars and destroys lives. If we do not cut the rate of crime, the number of victims will continue escalating at an alarming pace. The lives of those who have turned toward better behavior will continue to be wasted, their families will continue to suffer, and the circle of victims will continue to expand.

Even if I were not a priest, even if Barbara had not passed over and I was practicing law or working in academe, I would be promoting that Americans change their criminal justice system so that we can return to the origins of our legal professions. Ours is not to punish. Ours is to heal and to make amends.

In my life, I have learned that when we begin a journey for the right reasons, we do not need to know every single step we will take along the way. An honorable beginning ensures that the journey will unfold as it is meant to unfold. And so I do not believe that it is essential that we nail down each and every minuscule provision for the Crime Peace Plan. It is essential only that we begin, and begin now.

For the question is not whether the Crime Peace Plan will work. The only question is whether there are legislators, prosecutors, defense counsel, judges, prison administrators, probation officers, and concerned citizens brave—or crazy—enough to believe that, together, we can change the system.

Let us hope and pray that this is so.

—FR. DAVE LINK

Acknowledgments

My gratitude starts with you. You have stayed with me through the pages of a story that uplifts and inspires at the same time as it disrupts and dislodges. It takes courage to allow outdated conceptions and misconceptions to be modernized. I admire you for having given yourself up to the radical reorganization that is a side effect of getting to know Father Dave. You probably suspected early on that he would disturb some ideas and attitudes that were as comfortable as the threadbare slippers you cannot bring yourself to discard, and yet, you persisted. Thank you for trusting that the journey would be worth the shake-up.

I would be remiss if I did not ask the heroes and heroines of this book to take well-deserved curtain calls and bask for just a moment in the spotlight of these backpages.

Were it not for Superintendent William K. ("Bill") Wilson, this book would be only half a book, for it would lack the voices of the men who reside at Indiana State Prison. The fulcrum on which *Camerado* pivots is my access to the prisoners. This is a rare privilege, and it was made possible by Superintendent Wilson. For his trust in me and for his personal mentoring of this project, Superintendent Wilson has my deepest gratitude.

On April 29, 2010, *Camerado* was conceived in one electrifying moment. I am indebted to Mary Nucciarone, whose brief description of David Link changed the trajectory of my life. Thank you, Mary, for the word sketch that pierced my heart as if it were an arrow.

There are heroes, and there are superheroes. Father Ted Hesburgh is a real-life superhero I never dreamed I would meet, let alone interview. Sitting in an iconic office with a world leader who has fought for the things I hold to be most precious in life— peace, equality, morality, education, and justice—I felt as if I were talking to one of God's personal assistants. Father Ted was gracious, patient, and erudite. He taught me that the taping of an interview is not an imposition but a sign of respect. In his honor, I named the digital recording device I bought immediately following our first interview "Hesburgh." Thank you, Father Ted, for your time, for the benedictions you prayed on behalf of my work and me, and for the glory you so generously donated to my book.

The Most Reverend Bishop Dale J. Melczek helped me understand just how ordained the ordainment of David T. Link really is. I am grateful, Bishop Melczek, for the insights into Father Dave and his mission that you shared with me.

I am grateful to Father Jim McDonald for making some key law school experiences come alive for me. Neither of us suspected that a little remark he tossed out with a chuckle near the end of our interview would prove to be a diamond in the rough. It was late in the writing process when I mined this little gem and placed it at the end of the final chapter. Thank you, Father McDonald, for giving me the Brooklyn Bridge.

I am indebted to Lou Nanni for an incisive interview. After our time was up and the Hesburgh recorder had been turned off, Mr. Nanni invited me to follow him down the hallway as he rushed to his next meeting so that we could extend our conversation another couple of minutes. I tossed out a big question: With the socio-political systems in America so broken, and knowing that there are limited resources, where do we begin? Do we start with the family? The educational system? Where? Mr. Nanni stopped in his tracks and turned the full force of his piercing blue eyes upon me. No, he said, our society cannot be healed if we approach its brokenness *systemically*. It is up to each one of us to become an active participant. Then, and only then, will we begin to resolve our most crushing problems. I think that Mr. Nanni has it exactly right.

I am grateful to effervescent Steve Camilleri for showing me around the Center for the Homeless at South Bend (cfh.net), of which he is justifiably proud. This outreach model offers every community a vivid example of how to create an oasis of healing and restoration. For citizens who are struggling with the crippling effects of poverty, homelessness, substance or behavior addictions, lack of education, joblessness, and purposelessness, this model kindles hope.

I am grateful to Captain Bill McLean for taking me inside the Camelot-esque aura of the Dave Link era. Then, everything that Nancy and Tom Shaffer talked about buttressed this impression of a remarkable period in the history of the Notre Dame Law School. Dean Link's former students, including but not limited to Patrick Brennan, Elton Johnson, Jim Dahl, and Rich Hill, made me feel as if I had been inside the classrooms that had prepared them for the courtrooms and boardrooms of their futures. I am grateful to all of Father Dave's friends, colleagues, associates, and former students who entrusted me with their memories of a singular place and time in their lives.

I am deeply grateful to David, Mary, Maureen, Teran and their families for their kindness and cooperation. I appreciate your gracious willingness to allow the book to assume whatever shape was necessary so that the most essential of your father's messages could be conveyed. This, despite the fact that the family-oriented memories I had written in meticulous and loving detail were cut, carved, and whittled away—an unfortunate consequence of the publishing process, for which I beg your forgiveness. Best experience: pizza at Rocco's. It sure was fun watching the expressions on the faces of the other diners as two generations of Links addressed the Roman Catholic priest sitting at the head of the table "Dad" and "Papa."

To Father Dave's sister, the inimitable Miss Dody, I extend my heartfelt thanks. For the record: I agree with you that your baby brother is indeed exceptional in every way.

I am profoundly grateful to Barbara Ann Link for the selflessness with which she shared her husband with the rest of the world, and for being his inspiration. I wish I had known her.

My long-lost college pal Patty Warner Kerston offered sage advice very early on. In suggesting that I channel Barbara Link in writing this book, my astute friend was right on the money. For this and many other reasons, I'm so glad I found you, Patty.

I am grateful to Ira Glass (thisamericanlife.org), who handed me the key to the inner sanctum of the story when he told me to "find the movement."

Assistant Director Sue Shidler and her staff at Hammes Notre Dame Bookstore have been ardent supporters of this project from its inception. When I learned that Sue had known and admired Dave Link for years, I made a little pilgrimage to her gloriously cluttered office each time I was on campus, and we talked. I soon grew to love this sunny woman so gifted in the art of mothering people. When Sue indicated that she would like to read the manuscript, I sent her a digital copy, which she read, lacking a laptop or iPad, on her *cell phone*! She loved talking about being the first to shelve *Camerado,* and about the book release event and home football game signings she planned on hosting at the bookstore. Tragically, this was not to be. After having been gravely ill for many years, Sue lost a heroic battle against cancer on April 22, 2013. The world seems a much dimmer place without Sue's megawatt smile.

Jeanine Donaldson, director of my beloved Elyria Y.W.C.A. (ywcaelyria.org), has provided contagious enthusiasm and far-reaching support for this, the latest in a series of projects I have dragged her into. It is my privilege to walk in friendship beside Jeanine in a quest to sponsor justice and equality where they are in short supply.

Without Bonnie Stadnik and the entire Avon Commons Heinen's crew, my family and I would have starved to death long ago. Tri and Tammy Nguyen, my favorite fellow vegans, make me feel as if I am somebody special every time I walk in their door. For years, loyal, cheerful, talented Mark Thomas has been ready to help me look my best. My long-suffering guitar teacher, Chuck Smolko, has the patience of a saint; I owe him hours and hours of practice time. I am fortunate to have the friendship and expert assistance of Randy Zinn (msmctech.com), who is responsible for my terrific website. I am grateful to my high school friend David Cameron Anderson for capturing a terrific jacket cover photo.

A special note of gratitude must be sounded for Julianne

Zagrans, Esq., as fine a research assistant as any author has ever had, and to Jackie Zagrans, LMFT, who was my go-to expert for mental health issues. I am deeply grateful for the compelling visual storytelling and promotional work done by Brittany Morehouse (onemanbandreporter.com).

The fact that I am a Random House author inspires many pinch-me moments. I simply cannot believe that I'm 2-for-2 with this superior publishing house. In the world of sports, this would be like playing in the World Series and batting 1.000. I am deeply grateful for all the ways that *Camerado* benefitted from the peerless professionalism given by Johanna Inwood, Steve Cobb, Carie Freimuth, Katie Moore, Cathy Hennessy, and Lindsay Olson. Copy editor Maggie Carr, as fine a clean-up batter as can be found in the industry, once again provided my work a winning assist.

I never thought I'd go to prison. I certainly didn't want to. I only went for the sake of my book. I was stunned when the experience proved to be both transformative and fulfilling. I discovered that people who live on the other side of razor wire are, bottom line, people. Like everyone, they have a story to tell. They have a past, a present, and a future, hopes and dreams, regrets and sorrows, answered and unanswered prayers. To my great surprise, every time I went to prison, I couldn't wait to go back.

I shall never forget participating in the Native American worship service, where I was privileged to be welcomed into the Circle and where I observed Chief Standing Bear Hayes in action. I thank Bear and his amazing wife, Tricia Teater, for their selfless sharing: big bows to you both. I am grateful to my "secretary," Jeff Krumm, for keeping my interviews running smoothly as well as for his diligent guardianship, and his candid insights.

Every time I attended Mass at Indiana State Prison, I looked forward to hearing Bill Dixon (he really does sound just like Eddie Vedder) and David Parrish, whose music always moves me to tears. Thank you, Bill and David, for your kindness, friendship, and honesty. David, I owe you extra special thanks for the beauty and grace that your dream sequence, your quotes, and your lyrics brought to this book. Thank you, thank you, my friend. And to *all* of the men at Indiana State Prison, even if your interviews did not make it into the book, I want you to know that you have my heartfelt gratitude. I promise that I will never forget you.

I am indebted to the exemplary leadership at Westville Correction Facility, including Superintendent Mark Levenhagen, Assistant Superintendent Andrew Pazera, Administrative Assistant Dave Leonard, Major Dan Forker, and Recreation Supervisor Bill Breen for two spectacular days spent on the Westville campus. To Marvin Simms and Andy Pulver, I extend my very deepest thanks. You were absolutely wonderful.

I thank Judy Jellicoe and all of the men at the South Bend reentry facility who shared their stories with me. Gary Sparkman deserves a special shout-out for making Father Dave (and me) so very proud. Keep up the good work, Gary. Miracles look good on you.

If ever my reserves were running low, I had only to reach into my family-and-friends vault and suddenly I was good as gold. Gavin Poston has been a source of encouragement and tower of strength throughout my journey. That he has evolved from being my buddy and defender to a heck of a publicist touches the heart of this little sis. My heart is full to overflowing with gratitude for my Little Loves, Keiran Siobhan and Devon Fiona, whose kisses and hugs and pink-and-purple happiness light up my life. Suzy Poston, Candy Zagrans Day, Dave Merriman, Justin Stark, Amanda Halstead, Kathy and Mark Wainwright, fellow writer Dawn Neely-Randall, Mary Ellen Brock, Mary and Mark Gigliotti, Sharon DeSanto, Kathy Skerritt, my three Kims (Kim Brody, Kim Foisy, and Kim Miraldi), Bonnie Bowerman, Carol Jaworski and all my book-loving friends in Sunday Night Solstice Book Club, Tim (my) Moore, Tim Slager, Ronald Lane, George Rossi, Mark Ballard, Debbie Harrison-Rössner, Cartie and John Antonelli, my favorite piping firefighter, Patrick Coleman, and, of course, Donovan never fail to provide me the companionship, care, concern, and prayers I need. I thank each one of you for your sustaining camaraderie.

My family is and always will be the center of my universe. Eric, Brittany, Robby, Jackie, Juli, Connor, and Dillon: you are my core group of camerados. Without you, I am but a faint shadow of myself. With you, for you, and because of you, I can do anything. For your abiding love and friendship, I give you my heart.

For two years I listened as men and women of all ages and walks of life struggled to put into words the affection, admiration, awe, and gratitude they felt for a man of many monikers. Now it is my turn, and I feel like a kindergartner with too few crayons to draw the picture I see in my mind's eye.

Father Dave, for letting me tag along into the corners of your world, the heart of your memories, and the essence of your experience, I thank you. For the healing love you have infused into the universe, I thank you. For your trust in my abilities, I thank you. Though you have been climbing sociologic mountains for more than fifty years, your eyes still light up when faced with new challenges, and so the two of us had a good time scaling a few ranges together. I love that each time we stood upon a summit you always cast your gaze upward and outward, never behind. In the beginning, there was that enigmatic moment in which you decided that the Holy Spirit was behind this whole thing, that it was She who had put the two of us together. In the middle, there is this crystalline anteroom in which we now stand, holding this hopeful book in our hands. At the end of this work that we have done together, another journey beckons. Camerado, I give you my pledge that I will continue this journey with you, for you, and in your honor.

As for my Camerado-in-Chief, Gary Jansen, the man without whom this book would never have happened, if there are words that can express the profundity of my gratitude, I have not yet learned them.

From the very first, Gary believed in and championed both my project and me. He helped me shape the contours of a number of drafts (which I refuse to count). I learned with each successive draft that the more impossible his directive, the more essential it was to achieve it. I am the luckiest of the lucky to have been blessed with this consummate editor who cared enough to keep pushing me further and further into my own abilities until, at last, I found myself stepping out of the way and holding the door open to the truest and most elegant essence of the story. For your fiery devotion and fiercely protective guardianship, Gary, I give you, now and forever, my very best work.

I am one of eight children born to parents who were amazing, exemplary, and empowering. Growing up in a family with five brothers and two sisters has been one of the greatest blessings of my life. On September 8, 1975, however, God took two of my brothers Home. Sitting side-by-side in the car my brother Bruce had so generously given to his younger siblings, Rob, who was then twenty-two years old, and Steven, who was only nineteen, died instantly in a head-on car collision. I have been missing them ever since.

Yet God found a way to ease my sorrow. As is written in John 14:27:

> *Peace I leave with you, My peace I give to you; not as the world gives do I give to you. Let not your heart be troubled, neither let it be afraid.*

God sent me another little brother. He came to me in the guise of an editor but his true identity was revealed in the course of writing this book.

My new younger brother is someone who shines in the golden tradition of cohesive, inexpressible relationships between editors and authors. I'm no Steinbeck, yet I was blessed with a Covici.

To my unending delight, my new brother loves all things Kerouacian, just as I do.

He is someone with whom I can share this wonderful adventure we call life. He is a fellow photographer and a coconspirator in my relentless pursuit of good music. He is someone with whom I can laugh and cry, hope and dream, read and discuss, work and write. Someone whose family feels like Family.

And so, Camerado-in-Chief, I give you my hand. My friendship. My loyalty. My love.

And my book.

Notes

PART ONE: COURAGE

One-Way Train Overture

22 **"Almost all of the men I counsel":** "The Fatherless Generation," The Fatherless Generation, Father Factor in Incarceration, accessed November 17, 2012.

22 **"Most of them have suffered physical, emotional, or sexual
abuse":** Ibid.

22 **"Almost all are victims of crushing poverty":** "Improving
the Educational Skills of Jail Inmates Preliminary Program
Findings." Accessed November 14, 2012.

22 **"Fully 60 to 75 percent":** "Reading, Literacy & Educational Statistics—The Literacy Company." Speed Reading,
Reading Software—Improve Your Reading Speed, Com-
prehension and Recall—The Literacy Company. Accessed
February 7, 2012.

22 **"In fact, there is a direct correlation":** Caroline Wolf
Harlow, "Education and Correctional Populations," Bureau
of Justice Statistics Special Report, U.S. Department of
Justice, January 2003.

22 **For a country that prides itself:** Human Rights Watch,
"World Report 2012: United States," January 2012,

http://www.hrw.org/world-report-2012/world-report
-2012-united-states.

22 **Her penal system is the largest:** Robert Perkinson, *Texas Tough: The Rise of America's Prison Empire* (New York: Metropolitan Books, 2010), introduction.

22 **More tax dollars are spent on corrections:** Vincent Shiraldi and Jason Ziedenberg, "The Punishing Decade: Prison and Jail Esimates at the Millennium," *Justice Policy Institute.* May 1, 2000, http://justicepolicy.org /research/2064.

22 **The majority of Father Dave's brothers:** Michael Jacobson-Hardy, "Behind the Razor Wire," in *Behind the Razor Wire: Portrait of a Contemporary American Prison System* (New York: New York University Press, 1998), 10–12; Michelle Alexander, *The New Jim Crow: Mass Incarceration in the Age of Colorblindness* (New York: New Press, 2010).

22 **The two-thirds recidivism rate:** The Pew Charitable Trusts, "Public Safety, Public Spending: Forecasting America's Prison Population 2007–2011," February 14, 2007, http://www.pewtrusts.org/uploaded files /wwwpewtrustsorg/Reports/State-based_policy/PSPP _prison_projections_0207.pdf; Jennifer Laudano, The Pew Charitable Trusts, "Pew Finds Four in 10 Offenders Return to Prison Within Three Years," April 12, 2011, http://www.pewtrusts.org/news_room_detail.aspx?id =85899358607. Accessed November 16, 2012.

22 **Some of the old-timers confided:** The Pew Charitable Trusts, "Public Safety, Public Spending."

23 **"They say it's a Department of Corrections":** Alexander, *The New Jim Crow*; William J. Wilson, *More than Just Race: Being Black and Poor in the Inner City* (New York: W. W. Norton, 2009); Loïc Wacquant, *Punishing the Poor: The Neoliberal Government of Social Insecurity* (Durham, NC: Duke University Press, 2009).

PART TWO: COMMUNITY

Prison as Community

74 **One of Indiana State Prison's cell houses:** Rick A. Richards, "Indiana State Prison a Part of Michigan City History," *The Beacher Weekly Newspaper* (Michigan City), May 20, 2010, http://www.bluestreakim.com/Beacher May20.pdf.

PART THREE: COMPASSION

9. The Compassion Crucible

164 **Researchers estimate that between 15 and 35 percent:** Kent A. Kiehl and Joshua W. Buckholtz, "Inside the Mind of a Psychopath," *Scientific American* 21, no. 4 (September/ October 2010): 24, http://cicn.vanderbilt.edu/images /news/psycho.pdf.

164 **Add a negative environment:** Ibid., 27–28.

169 **Second, the feeling of guilt:** James Gilligan, "Pictures of

Pain: The Criminality of the Criminal Justice System,"
in *Behind the Razor Wire: Portrait of a Contemporary American Prison System* (New York: New York University Press,
1999), 30–34; Robin Karr-Morse and Meredith S.
Wiley, *Ghosts from the Nursery: Tracing the Roots of Violence*
(New York: Atlantic Monthly Press, 1997), esp. "Grand
Central: Early Brain Anatomy and Violence" and "Baby,
Get Your Gun: The Impact of Trauma and Head
Injury."

Afterword: A Crime Peace Plan

226 **In 2008 the United States incarcerated 2.3 million people:**
Staff writers, "10 Stats You Should Know About Our
Prison System," criminaljusticeusa.com, May 17, 2011,
http://www.criminaljusticeusa.com/blog/2011/10-stats
-you-should-know-about-our-prison-system.

227 **In the state of Illinois, for example, a "seven-month investigation":** Hilary Hurd Anyaso, "The High Cost of Wrongful Convictions in Illinois: Dollars Wasted, Lives Lost and
Ruined, Justice Run Amok: A Landmark Investigation,"
Northwestern University News, June 20, 2011, http://
www.northwestern.edu/newscenter/stories/2011/06
/wrongful-conviction-cost.html. Accessed December 2,
2011.

231 **Judges and lawyers would do well to remember their origins:** Warren E. Burger, "Remarks of Warren E. Burger
Chief Justice of the United States at the Dedication of
Notre Dame London Law Centre: The Role of the Law-

yer Today London, England, Friday, July 29, 1983." *Notre Dame Law Review* 59, no. 1 (1983–1984).

233 **For instance, prosecutors can use the threat of felonies:** See Dan Thomason at thomasondan@aol.com

237 **"Some actions that would cause the typical American":** Staff writers, "10 Stats You Should Know About Our Prison System," criminaljusticeusa.com, May 17, 2011, http://www.criminaljusticeusa.com/blog/2011/10-stats -you-should-know-about-our-prison-system.

247 **To be eligible for nomination, an incarcerated person must be free of a Class A violation:** In Indiana, while incarcerated, Violation of Law; Assault (with a weapon); Rioting; Possession of Dangerous/Deadly Contraband/Property; Escape; Conspiracy/Attempting/Aiding or Abetting; Trafficking; Nonconsensual Sexual Act Against a Visitor, Another Offender, or Staff; Refusing a Mandatory Program; Assault on Staff; or Violation of Condition of Temporary Leave.

247 **and free of a Class B violation:** In Indiana, while incarcerated, Possession or Use of a Controlled Substance; Refusal to submit to Testing; Abusive Sexual Contact Against Staff, Visitor or Another Offender; Possession of Electronic Device; Security Threat Group/Unauthorized Organizational Activity; Impairment of Surveillance; Assault/Battery; Threatening; Unauthorized Possession of Property; Sexual Conduct; Possession of Plans for Weapons; Possession of Escape Paraphernalia; Arson; Group Demonstration/Work Stoppage; Tampering with Lock; Possession of Altered Property; Counterfeit Docu-

ments; Intoxicants; Bribing/Giving; Fleeing/Resisting; Disorderly Conduct; Conspiracy/Attempting Aiding or Abetting; Filing Frivolous Claims, Possession of Offensive Material, or Possession or Solicitation of Unauthorized Personal Information.

Suggested Reading

Albom, Mitch. *Have a Little Faith: A True Story*. New York: Hyperion, 2009.

Alexander, Michelle. *The New Jim Crow: Mass Incarceration in the Age of Colorblindness*. New York, NY: New Press, 2010.

Berlin, Isaiah, ed. Henry Hardy. *Freedom and Its Betrayal: Six Enemies of Human Liberty*. Princeton, NJ: Princeton University Press, 2002.

Frampton, Mary Louise, Ian Haney Lopez, and Jonathan Simon. *After the War on Crime: Race, Democracy, and a New Reconstruction*. New York: New York University Press, 2008.

Frankl, Viktor E. *Man's Search for Meaning*. Boston: Beacon Press, 2006.

Gandhi, Mohandas Karamchand, Mahadev Haribhai Desai, and Sissela Bok. *Autobiography: The Story of My Experiments with Truth*. Boston: Beacon Press, 1993.

Gilligan, James. *Preventing Violence*. London: Thames & Hudson, 2001.

———. *Violence: Reflections on a National Epidemic*. New York: Vintage Books, 1996.

Hesburgh, Theodore Martin, and Jerry Reedy. *God, Country, Notre Dame: The Autobiography of Theodore M. Hesburgh*. New York: Doubleday, 1990.

Jacobson-Hardy, Michael. *Behind the Razor Wire: Portrait of a*

Contemporary American Prison System. New York: New York University Press, 1999.

Karr-Morse, Robin, and Meredith S. Wiley. *Ghosts from the Nursery: Tracing the Roots of Violence.* New York: Atlantic Monthly Press, 1997.

King, Martin Luther. *The Measure of a Man.* Philadelphia: Fortress Press, 1988.

King, Martin Luther, and James Melvin Washington. *A Testament of Hope: The Essential Writings and Speeches of Martin Luther King, Jr.* San Francisco: HarperCollins, 1991.

Kotlowitz, Alex. *The Other Side of the River: A Story of Two Towns, a Death, and America's Dilemma.* New York: Anchor Books, Random House, 1998.

———. *There Are No Children Here: The Story of Two Boys Growing Up in the Other America.* New York: Anchor Books, Random House, 1991.

Lee, Harper. *To Kill a Mockingbird.* New York: Harper Perennial Classic, 2002.

Lewis, John. *Across That Bridge: Life Lessons and a Vision for Change.* New York: Hyperion, 2012.

Masters, Jarvis Jay. *That Bird Has My Wings: The Autobiography of an Innocent Man on Death Row.* New York: HarperOne, 2009.

Mauer, Marc. *Race to Incarcerate.* New York: New Press, 1999.

McNeil, Brenda Salter, and Rick Richardson. *The Heart of Racial Justice: How Soul Change Leads to Social Change.* Downers Grove, IL: InterVarsity Press, 2004.

Neihardt, John G. *Black Elk Speaks: Being the Life Story of a Holy Man of the Oglala Sioux.* Lincoln, NE: University of Nebraska Press, 2005.

Nurse, Anne. *Fatherhood Arrested: Parenting from Within the Juvenile Justice System*. Nashville, TN: Vanderbilt University Press, 2002.

————. *Locked Up, Locked Out: Young Men in the Juvenile Justice System*. Nashville, TN: Vanderbilt University Press, 2010.

O'Brien, Michael. *Hesburgh: A Biography*. Washington, D.C.: Catholic University of America Press, 1998.

Payne, Ruby K. *A Framework for Understanding Poverty*. Highlands, TX: Aha! Process, 2005.

Peltier, Leonard F. ed. Harvey Arden. *Prison Writings: My Life Is My Sun Dance*. New York: St. Martin's, 1999.

Perkinson, Robert. *Texas Tough: The Rise of America's Prison Empire*. New York: Metropolitan Books, 2010.

Pettit, Becky. *Invisible Men: Mass Incarceration and the Myth of Black Progress*. New York: Russell Sage Foundation, 2012.

Phillips, Jenny. *Letters from the Dhamma Brothers: Meditation Behind Bars*. Onalaska, WA: Pariyatti Publishing, 2008.

Prejean, Helen. *Dead Man Walking: An Eyewitness Account of the Death Penalty in the United States*. New York: Vintage Books, 1994.

Rideau, Wilbert. *In the Place of Justice: A Story of Punishment and Deliverance*. New York: Alfred A. Knopf, 2010.

Shere, Dennis. *Cain's Redemption: A Story of Hope and Transformation in America's Bloodiest Prison*. Chicago: Northfield Publishing, 2005.

Söring, Jens. *The Convict Christ: What the Gospel Says About Criminal Justice*. Maryknoll, NY: Orbis Books, 2006.

————. *An Expensive Way to Make Bad People Worse: An Essay on Prison Reform from an Insider's Perspective*. New York: Lantern Books, 2004.

U.S. Conference of Catholic Bishops. *Responsibility, Rehabilitation and Restoration: A Catholic Perspective on Crime and Criminal Justice.* Washington, D.C.: U.S. Conference of Catholic Bishops, November 15, 2000.

Van Ness, Daniel W., and Karen Heetderks Strong. *Restoring Justice: An Introduction to Restorative Justice.* New Providence, NJ: LexisNexis, 2010.

Wacquant, Loïc J. D. *Punishing the Poor: The Neoliberal Government of Social Insecurity.* Durham, NC: Duke University Press, 2009.

Wilkerson, Isabel. *The Warmth of Other Suns: The Epic Story of America's Great Migration.* New York, NY: Random House, 2010.

Wilson, William J. *More than Just Race: Being Black and Poor in the Inner City.* New York: W. W. Norton, 2009.

Zehr, Howard. *The Little Book of Restorative Justice.* Intercourse, PA: Good Books, 2002.